WIT & WISDOM
OF
ABRAHAM LINCOLN

WIT & WISDOM
OF
ABRAHAM LINCOLN

As Reflected in His Letters and Speeches

Edited by H. Jack Lang

STACKPOLE
BOOKS

Published 2006 by:
Stackpole Books
5067 Ritter Road
Mechanicsburg, PA 17055-6921
www.stackpolebooks.com

Published in the United States of America
Previously published by Greenberg Publishers

10 9 8 7 6 5 4 3 2

Cover design by Wendy A. Reynolds

Library of Congress Cataloging-in-Publication Data

Lincoln, Abraham, 1809–1865.
    The wit and wisdom of Abraham Lincoln as reflected in his briefer
letters and speeches / edited by H. Jack Lang.
        p. cm.
    Originally published: New York : Greenberg Publishers, c1941.
    ISBN 0-8117-0160-3 (pbk. : alk. paper)
    1. Lincoln, Abraham, 1809–1865—Quotations. 2. Lincoln, Abra-
ham, 1809–1865—Correspondence. 3. Speeches, addresses, etc.,
American. 4. Quotations, American. 5. American letters. I. Lang, H.
Jack, 1904– II. Title.

    E457.92 2006
    081—dc22
                                                    2005056316
    ISBN 978-0-8117-0160-0

Contents

2. THE PRESIDENT (1861-1865)

Introduction

I

*All art does but consist in
the removal of surplusage.*
—WALTER PATER

"The artist," said Schiller, "may be known rather by what he *omits;* and in literature, too, the true artist may be best recognized by his tact of omission." Abraham Lincoln exercised this "tact of omission" to an amazing degree.

In the following pages an attempt has been made to collect, for the first time, Lincoln's masterpieces of brevity; the brevity which was not only the soul of his wit, but the sinew of his strength and the heart of his compassion.

Lincoln, said the *London Spectator,* could never tolerate the tyranny of mere words, but always pressed through them to the reality beyond. When Lincoln spoke he was an orator, never an elocutionist. Said Robert G. Ingersoll, in drawing this distinction:

"The elocutionists believe in the virtue of voice, the sublimity of syntax, the majesty of long sentences, and the genius of gesture.

"The orator loves the real, the simple, the natural. He places the thought above all. He knows that the greatest ideas should be expressed in the shortest words—that the greatest statues need the least drapery."

Lincoln's lessons in brevity began early. Everyone is familiar with the picture of gangling, young Abe, book in hand, stretched full-length before the fire, in his rough-hewn log-cabin. His first efforts at composition were written in charcoal, on the small area he was able to scrape clean on the back of a wood shovel. Paper was a precious commodity in the Lincoln household, and when young Abe was able to find a small scrap, he was forced "to cut his words close."

What formal education he had was picked up in "blab schools," where all writing and reading were done out loud. Lincoln never gave up this habit of reading out loud as he wrote, and as William E. Barton observed, "His verbal precision came in part from his weighing the word, both the sense and the sound, as he wrote it."

The subjects of Lincoln's study, as well as the manner, pointed toward a lucidity and conciseness of style. He formed a pattern of logic and clarity from his studies

[x]

of Euclid and he drank deeply from the "Grand Simplicities of the Bible."

His early legal training contributed, too. "In law," wrote Lincoln to Usher F. Linder, "it is a good policy never to *plead* what you *need not,* lest you oblige yourself to *prove* what you *cannot."* Linder was the lawyer young Abe had once "let down" in a criminal case, by making a brief appeal when he was expected to make a very long one. "I shall never be old enough," said Lincoln on this and many later occasions, "to speak without embarrassment when I have nothing to say."

Throughout his whole life we find that brevity had an important influence on Lincoln. We learn, too, that it frequently served him as an evaluation of the merit of others. After reading one of the speeches General Grant had made to his army, Lincoln declared, "The modesty and brevity of that address shows that the officer issuing it . . . is the man to command."

When Henry Clay died in 1852 Lincoln said in his Eulogy:

"Mr. Clay's eloquence did not consist, as many fine specimens of eloquence do, of types and figures, of antithesis and elegant arrangement of words and sentences, but rather of that deeply earnest and impassioned tone and manner which can proceed only from great sincerity, and a thorough conviction in the speaker of the justice and importance of his

[xi]

cause. This it is that truly touches the chords of sympathy; and those who heard Mr. Clay never failed to be moved by it, or ever afterward forgot the impression. All his efforts were made for practical effect. He never spoke merely to be heard."

Having little of the magniloquent in his own nature Lincoln had little patience when he found it in others. When he read an unnecessarily long and verbose brief a lawyer had prepared, Lincoln remarked,—"It's like the lazy preacher that used to write long sermons, and the explanation was, he got to writin' and was too lazy to stop."

There are many incidents reminiscent of the great philosopher Pascal who once apologized to a friend for having written a twenty-page letter, saying that he had "no leisure to make it shorter." General Cameron, Lincoln's first Secretary of War, wrote the President-Elect in 1860, "You may as well be getting your inaugural address ready, so as to have plenty of time to make it short."

Even in formal state papers, Lincoln believed in saying what he had to say in the fewest possible words, without frills or ornamentation of any kind. "What a sharpshooter's bead he could draw in one sentence," said Carl Sandburg who related the story of one occasion when Secretary of State Seward suggested that Lincoln's message to the British Prime Minister could be couched in more diplomatic terms, to befit that dignitary's lofty station. Said Mr. Lincoln:

"Mr. Secretary, do you suppose Palmerston will understand our position from my letter, just as it is?"

"Certainly, Mr. President."

"Do you suppose the London *Times* will?"

"Certainly."

"Do you suppose the average Englishman of affairs will?"

"Certainly. It cannot be mistaken in England."

"Do you suppose that a hackman on his box will understand it?"

"Very readily, Mr. President."

"Very well, Mr. Secretary, I guess we'll let her slide just as she is."

There is evidence after evidence that brevity of style was not only inborn in Abraham Lincoln but that it was an objective which he assiduously pursued. He concluded a terse note to John Bennett by saying, "This is not a long letter but it contains the whole story."

Lincoln's *Wit and Wisdom* makes fascinating reading because he was a master of the art of economizing your—the reader's—time. There is no extraneous verbiage to cloud the light of his shining truths. The Cambridge History of American Literature's seventeen-page tribute to Lincoln's writings testifies that they will forever rank among the world's models of brevity. Their greatness is best summed up by Harriet Beecher Stowe:

"We say of Lincoln's writing, that for all true, manly purposes of writing, there are passages in his state papers that could not be better put—they are absolutely perfect. They are brief, condensed, intense, and with a power of insight and expression which make them worthy to be inscribed in letters of gold."

II

And when he fell in whirlwind, he went down
As when a kingly cedar green with boughs,
Goes down with a great shout upon the hills,
And leaves a lonesome space against the sky.
—EDWIN MARKHAM

Abraham Lincoln left "a lonesome place against the sky," but his words live on because their ringing truths were not for the ears of his age alone.

"I am little inclined to say anything unless I hope to produce some good by it," wrote Lincoln. It is because of this determination that we find so much meaningful counsel compressed into every sentence he uttered or wrote.

Lincoln's words were words of wisdom whether he was advising a faltering general, a shiftless stepbrother, an influential newspaper editor, or a young man struggling to make his way in the world.

Lincoln, the lawyer, the father, the leader of his country, asked himself the same questions we are asking ourselves today. "What is Democracy?" queried Lincoln and then proceeded to give an admirable definition in two short sentences.

"Shall the liberties of this country be preserved?" wondered Lincoln and then told the assembled citizens of Indianapolis, "When the people rise in mass in behalf of the liberties of this country, truly it may be said, 'The gates of hell cannot prevail against them.'"

"It has long been a grave question," observed Lincoln on another occasion, "whether any government, not too strong for the liberties of its people, can be strong enough to maintain its existence in great emergencies." The answer Lincoln found not in material resources but in the resolute spirit of the American people. "Gold is good in its place, but living, brave, patriotic men are better than gold."

So amazingly applicable to present conditions are the observations of Lincoln that we find it difficult to believe they were uttered for any time but our own. Is it really Lincoln, and not a contemporary, who said that when the "Know-Nothings," who preached the doctrine of racial hatred, should come into control, "I shall prefer emigrating to some country where they make no pretense of loving liberty,—to Russia, for instance, where despotism can be taken pure, and without the base alloy of hypocrisy."

Is Lincoln not speaking of our own fifth-columnists when he writes John W. Crisfield decrying the attitude of the courts in finding "a safe place for certain men to stand on the Constitution, whilst they should stab it in another place." Again, when a minister used his pulpit to preach un-American doctrines, Lincoln instructed General Curtis: "When an individual in a church or out of it becomes dangerous to the public interest, he must be checked; but let the churches, as such, take care of themselves.

There is hardly a modern problem which Lincoln has not thought through for us with his great and good judgment. He recognized the "hard dilemma" which every conscientious objector and true pacifist faces, opposed as he is, "on principle and faith," to both war and oppression. In his inspired letter of September 4, 1864 he answers this perplexing question not only for Eliza P. Gurney of the Quaker Society of Friends but for all conscientious objectors to come.

Lincoln's wisdom is not only revealed in his judgments on the great issues of the day but in his counsel on everyday affairs. Lincoln was always a keen student of human psychology. His letters to his generals comprise a comprehensive study in the strategy of handling people. He knew just when to be firm and unyielding, when to praise or to censure, and when to be humbly apologetic to gain his end.

In his famous letter to "Fighting Joe" Hooker, Lincoln knew he could safely say, "I have heard, in such a way as to believe it, of your recently saying that both the army and the government needed a dictator. What I now ask of you is military success, and I will risk the dictatorship." To the complaining General Hunter he admonished, "He who does *something* at the head of one Regiment, will eclipse him who does *nothing* at the head of a hundred."

In a gentler vein he could chide General McClellan for his over-cautiousness and inaction, or write letters of encouragement and grateful appreciation. Most remarkable of his expressions of gratitude were those written not in appreciation of successes gained, but in dark hours of defeat, when he knew that his generals had exerted their best efforts. His letters to Gustavus Fox, who failed in his attempt to provision Fort Sumter; to General Meade, who failed to pursue his advantage after Gettysburg; and to the Army of the Potomac after their crushing defeat at Fredericksburg, best show Lincoln's sympathetic understanding.

Among Lincoln's earlier writings we find many examples of his unfailing sense of humor—his "rat-hole" letter to a New York firm, his soap testimonial to Professor Gardner, his much-quoted letter to little Grace Bedell—to name just a few. It is a commentary on his greatness of spirit that in later years, even in times of most serious crises, his sense of humor never deserted him.

Lincoln's instinctive faculty for finding the right word for every occasion makes his letters and speeches a source of inspiration and guidance for everyone. His letters of consolation are classic examples for all to follow—not only the famous note to Mrs. Bixby, but those to the parents of Colonel Ellsworth and to the daughter of Colonel McCullough. The same may be said of his letters of apology, acceptance, acknowledgment, and recommendation, for each is a perfect pattern of its type.

Acknowledgments

No collection of Lincoln's writings would be possible were it not for the "spade work" of those who ferreted out his precious documents from collectors' albums, dealers' shelves, newspaper morgues, and library and government archives. The first seven important works listed below—upon which this editor has drawn heavily —include virtually all of Lincoln's known writings. A debt of gratitude is due to: Dr. Louis A. Warren, Director, and M. A. Cook, Librarian, of The Lincoln National Life Foundation, for supplying a number of items hitherto unpublished in any of these standard works; Paul M. Angle, Librarian of The Illinois State Library in Springfield, for rendering needed assistance in checking the authenticity of certain letters and speeches included in this selection; Carl W. Schaefer, Cleveland lawyer and trustee of The Lincoln Memorial University, for offering helpful suggestions.

Complete Works of Abraham Lincoln (12 volumes). Edited by John G. Nicolay and John Hay. Tandy-Gettysburg Edition.

Uncollected Letters of Abraham Lincoln. By Gilbert A. Tracy. Houghton Mifflin Company.

Abraham Lincoln, A New Portrait, (2 volumes). By Emanuel Hertz. Horace Liveright, Inc.

New Letters and Papers of Lincoln. Compiled by Paul M. Angle. Houghton Mifflin Company.

Lincoln Letters, Hitherto Unpublished, In The Library of Brown University. The University Library.

Abraham Lincoln, The Prairie Years (2 volumes). By Carl Sandburg. Harcourt, Brace & Company.

Abraham Lincoln, The War Years (4 volumes). By Carl Sandburg. Harcourt, Brace & Company.

The Real Lincoln. By Jesse W. Weik. Houghton Mifflin Company.

Abraham Lincoln and The Hooker Letter. By William E. Barton. The Bowling Green Press.

The Life and Writings of Abraham Lincoln. By Philip Van Doren Stern. Random House.

~~~~~~

". . . short and sweet like the old woman's dance."

~~~~~~

L*INCOLN'S first political speech, as later remembered by his friend A. Y. Ellis, was the very essence of brevity. It won respect for Young Abe but not the election—the only time he ever was defeated by popular vote.*

FIRST POLITICAL SPEECH
AT PAPPSVILLE, ILL.—MARCH, 1832

F ELLOW-CITIZENS:

I presume you all know who I am. I am humble Abraham Lincoln. I have been solicited by many friends to become a candidate for the Legislature. My politics are short and sweet, like the old woman's dance. I am in favor of a national bank. I am in favor of the internal improvement system, and a high protective tariff. These are my sentiments and political principles. If elected, I shall be thankful; if not it will be all the same.

Lincoln — The Postmaster

IN 1833 *Lincoln served as postmaster of the small town of New Salem. He accepted this federal post, which none of his fellow townsmen wanted, so that he could read the newspapers. These pointed words were addressed to a publisher who demanded a postage receipt.*

LETTER TO GEORGE SPEARS

Circa 1833

MR. SPEARS:

At your request I send you a receipt for the postage on your paper. I am somewhat surprised at your request. I will, however, comply with it. The law requires Newspaper postage to be paid in advance, and now that I have waited a full year you choose to wound my feelings by insinuating that unless you get a receipt I will probably make you pay it again.

Respectfully,

A. LINCOLN

Young Abe "Shows His Hand"

IN 1836 *Lincoln again ran for the State Legislature and once more stated his platform in the fewest possible words. This time he was elected by a comfortable majority.*

LETTER TO THE EDITOR OF THE *SANGAMON JOURNAL*

New Salem, June 13, 1836

TO THE EDITOR OF THE "JOURNAL":

In your paper of last Saturday I see a communication, over the signature of "Many Voters," in which the candidates who are announced in the "Journal" are called upon to "show their hands." Agreed. Here's mine.

I go for all sharing the privileges of the government who assist in bearing its burdens. Consequently, I go for admitting all whites to the right of suffrage who pay taxes or bear arms (by no means excluding females).

If elected, I shall consider the whole people of Sangamon my constituents, as well those that oppose as those that support me.

While acting as their representative, I shall be governed by their will on all subjects upon which I have the means of knowing what their will is; and upon all others, I shall do what my own judgment teaches me will best advance their interests. Whether elected or not, I go for distributing the proceeds of the sales of the public lands to the several States, to enable our State, in common with others, to dig canals and construct railroads without borrowing money and paying the interest on it.

If alive on the first Monday in November, I shall vote for Hugh L. White for President.

Very respectfully,

A. LINCOLN

~~~~~~

"... *let the worst come.*"

~~~~~~

WHEN *Colonel Robert Allen, opposing candidate for the Illinois Legislature, hinted that he "knew unspeakable things" about Lincoln and his running-mate, Lincoln challenged him to tell all.*

LETTER TO ROBERT ALLEN

New Salem, June 21, 1836

DEAR COLONEL:

I am told that during my absence last week you passed through this place, and stated publicly that you were in possession of a fact or facts which, if known to the public, would entirely destroy the prospects of N. W. Edwards and myself at the ensuing election; but that, through favor to us, you should forbear to divulge them. No one has needed favors more than I, and, generally, few have been less unwilling to accept them; but in this case favor to me would be injustice to the public, and therefore I must beg your pardon for declining it. That I once had the confidence of the people of Sangamon, is sufficiently evident; and if I have since done anything, either by design or misadventure, which if known would subject me to a forfeiture of that confidence, he that knows of that thing, and conceals it, is a traitor to his country's interest.

I find myself wholly unable to form any conjecture of what fact or facts, real or supposed, you spoke; but my opinion of your veracity will not permit me for a moment to doubt that you at least believed what you said. I am flattered with the personal regard you manifested for me; but I do hope that, on more mature reflection, you will view the public interest as a paramount consideration, and therefore determine to let the worst come. I here assure you that the candid statement of facts on your part, however low it may sink me, shall never break the tie of personal friendship between us. I wish an answer to this, and you are at liberty to publish both, if you choose.

Very respectfully,

A. LINCOLN

"Whatever woman may cast her lot with mine. . . ."

F*EW men have survived more bitter disappointments than did Abraham Lincoln. The one that nearly spelled his undoing was the death of Ann Rutledge in 1835. This great loss resulted in Lincoln's hypochondria and many impulsive reactions including his courting of Miss Mary Owens. We probably never shall know whether the realization that he was not truly in love or whether caution and a sense of fairness prompted this letter.*

LETTER TO MARY OWENS

Springfield, May 7, 1837

FRIEND MARY:

I have commenced two letters to send you before this, both of which displeased me before I got half done, and so I tore them up. The first I thought was not serious enough, and the second was on the other extreme. I shall send this, turn out as it may.

[7]

This thing of living in Springfield is rather a dull business, after all; at least it is to me. I am quite as lonesome here as I ever was anywhere in my life. I have been spoken to by but one woman since I have been here, and should not have been by her if she could have avoided it. I've never been to church yet, and probably shall not be soon. I stay away because I am conscious I should not know how to behave myself.

I am often thinking of what we said about your coming to live at Springfield. I am afraid you would not be satisfied. There is a great deal of flourishing about in carriages here, which it would be your doom to see without sharing it. You would have to be poor, without the means of hiding your poverty. Do you believe you could bear that patiently? Whatever woman may cast her lot with mine, should any ever do so, it is my intention to do all in my power to make her happy and contented; and there is nothing I can imagine that would make me more unhappy than to fail in the effort. I know I should be much happier with you than the way I am, provided I saw no signs of discontent in you. What you have said to me may have been in the way of jest, or I may have misunderstood it. If so, then let it be forgotten; if otherwise, I much wish you would think seriously before you decide. What I have said I will most positively abide by, provided you wish it. My opinion is that you had better not do it. You have not been accustomed to hardship, and it may be more severe than you now imagine. I know you are capable of thinking correctly on any subject, and if you deliberate maturely upon this before you decide, then I am willing to abide your decision.

You must write me a good long letter after you get this. You have nothing else to do, and though it might not seem interesting to you after you had written it, it would be a good deal of company to me in this "busy wilderness." Tell your sister I don't want to hear any more about selling out and moving. That gives me the "hypo" whenever I think of it.

Yours, etc.,

LINCOLN

~~~~~~

". . . like so many fish upon a trotline."

~~~~~~

RETURNING *from a visit to Kentucky, Lincoln writes to the sister of his friend "Josh" Speed, giving news of her brother's health and a vivid word picture of slaves being transported south.*

LETTER TO MARY SPEED

Bloomington, Ill., September 27, 1841

MY FRIEND:

Having resolved to write to some of your mother's family, and not having the express permission of anyone of them to do so, I have had some little difficulty in determining on which to inflict the task of reading what I now feel must be a most dull and silly letter; but when I remembered that you and I were something of cronies while I was at Farmington, and that while there I was under the necessity of shutting you up in a room to prevent your committing an assault and battery upon me, I instantly decided that you should be the devoted one. I assume that you have not heard from Joshua and myself since we left, because I think it doubtful whether he has written. You remember there was some uneasiness about Joshua's health when we left. That little indisposition of his turned out to be nothing serious, and it was pretty nearly forgotten when we reached Springfield. We got on board the steamboat Lebanon in the locks of the canal, about twelve o'clock M. of the day we left, and reached St. Louis the next Monday at 8 P. M. Nothing of interest happened during the passage, except the vexatious delays occasioned by the sand-bars be thought interesting. By the way, a fine example was presented on board the boat for contemplating the effect of condition upon human happiness. A gentleman had purchased twelve negroes in different parts of Kentucky, and was taking them to a farm in the South. They were chained six and six together. A small iron clevis was around the left wrist of each, and this was fastened to the main chain by a shorter one, at a convenient distance from the others, so that the negroes were strung together precisely like so many fish upon a trotline. In this condition they were being separated forever from the scenes of their childhood, their friends, their fathers and mothers, and brothers and sisters, and many of them from their wives and children, and going into perpetual slavery, where the lash of the master is proverbially more ruthless and unrelenting than any other where; and yet amid all these distressing circumstances, as we would think them, they were the most cheerful and apparently happy creatures on board. One whose offense for which he had been sold was an over-fondness for his wife, played the fiddle almost continually, and the others danced, sang, cracked jokes, and played various games with cards from day to day. How true it is that "God tempers the wind to the shorn lamb," or in other words, that he renders the worst of human conditions tolerable, while he permits the best to be nothing better than tolerable. To return to the narrative. When we reached Springfield, I stayed but one day, when I started on this tedious circuit where I now am. Do you remember my going to the city, while I was in Kentucky, to have a tooth extracted, and making a failure of it? Well, that same old tooth got to paining me so much that about a week since I had it torn out, bringing with it a bit of the jaw-bone, the consequence of which is that my mouth is now so sore that I can neither talk nor eat.

I am literally "subsisting on savory remembrances"—that is, being unable to eat, I am living upon the remembrance of the delicious dishes of peaches and cream we used to have at your house. When we left, Miss Fanny Henning was owing you a visit, as I understood. Has she paid it yet? If she has, are you not convinced that she is one of the sweetest girls in the world? There is but one thing about her, so far as I could perceive, that I would have otherwise than as it is—that is, something of a tendency to melancholy. This, let it be observed, is a misfortune, not a fault.

Give her an assurance of my very highest regard when you see her. Is little Siss Eliza Davis at your house yet? If she is, kiss her "o'er and o'er again" for me.

Tell your mother that I have not got her "present" (an "Oxford" Bible) with me, but I intend to read it regularly when I return home. I doubt not that it is really, as she says, the best cure for the blues, could one but take it according to the truth. Give my respects to all your sisters (including Aunt Emma) and brothers. Tell Mrs. Peay, of whose happy face I shall long retain a pleasant remembrance, that I have been trying to think of a name for her homestead, but as yet cannot satisfy myself with one. I shall be very happy to receive a line from you soon after you receive this, and in case you choose to favor me with one, address it to Charleston, Coles County, Ill., as I shall be there about the time to receive it. Your sincere friend,

A. LINCOLN

". . . groomsman to a man that has cut him out. . . ."

LINCOLN'S *first efforts toward election to Congress ended in disappointment. The Whigs determined upon his friend Edward D. Baker and then, somewhat ironically, elected Lincoln a delegate with instructions to vote for Baker.*

LETTER TO JOSHUA F. SPEED

Springfield, March 24, 1843

DEAR SPEED:
 . . . We had a meeting of the Whigs of the county here on last Monday to appoint delegates to a district convention; and Baker beat me, and got the delegation instructed to go for him. The meeting, in spite of my attempt to decline it, appointed me one of the delegates; so that in getting Baker the nomination I shall be fixed a good deal like a fellow who is made a groomsman to a man that has cut him out and is marrying his own dear "gal." About the prospects of your having a namesake at our town, can't say exactly yet.

A. LINCOLN

[15]

"As to speech-making. . . ."

SHORTLY *after he had taken his seat in Congress, Lincoln wrote home to Billy Herndon, his young law partner, confessing mild stage fright in addressing the House and discussing his aspirations to a second term.*

LETTER TO WILLIAM H. HERNDON

Washington, January 8, 1848

DEAR WILLIAM:
     Your letter of December 27 was received a day or two ago. I am much obliged to you for the trouble you have taken, and promise to take in my little business there. As to speechmaking, by way of getting the hang of the House I made a little speech two or three days ago on a post-office question of no general interest. I find speaking here and elsewhere about the same thing. I was about as badly scared, and no worse, as I am

when I speak in court. I expect to make one within a week or two, in which I hope to succeed well enough to wish you to see it.

It is very pleasant to learn from you that there are some who desire that I should be reëlected. I most heartily thank them for their kind partiality; and I can say, as Mr. Clay said of the annexation of Texas, that "personally I would not object" to a reëlection, although I thought at the time, and still think, it would be quite as well for me to return to the law at the end of a single term. I made the declaration that I would not be a candidate again, more from a wish to deal fairly with others, to keep peace among our friends, and to keep the district from going to the enemy, than for any cause personal to myself; so that, if it should so happen that nobody else wishes to be elected, I could not refuse the people the right of sending me again. But to enter myself as a competitor of others, or to authorize anyone so to enter me, is what my word and honor forbid.

I got some letters intimating a probability of so much difficulty amongst our friends as to lose us the district; but I remember such letters were written to Baker when my own case was under consideration, and I trust there is no more ground for such apprehension now than there was then. Remember I am always glad to receive a letter from you.

Most truly your friend,

A. LINCOLN

"the very best speech ... I ever heard."

FOR *myself," said Alexander Stephens in a speech before Congress, "I can only say, if the last funeral pile of liberty were lighted, I would mount it and expire in its flames before I would be coerced by any power, however great and strong, to sell or surrender the land of my home." These words, from the man who became vice president of the Confederacy, we find echoed in Lincoln's own speeches of later years.*

LETTER TO WILLIAM H. HERNDON

Washington, February 2, 1848

DEAR WILLIAM:

I just take my pen to say that Mr. Stephens, of Georgia, a little, slim, pale-faced, consumptive man, with a voice like Logan's, has just concluded the very best speech of an hour's length I ever heard. My old withered dry eyes are full of tears yet.

If he writes it out anything like he delivered it,
our people shall see a good many copies of it.

Yours truly,

A. LINCOLN

O N *one and the same sheet of paper Lincoln grants his father's request for $20 with a bit of good-natured chiding: and then refuses a larger amount to his step-brother, John D. Johnston, who was considering the possibility of supporting a wife, although a poor hand at providing for himself.*

LETTER TO THOMAS LINCOLN & JOHN D. JOHNSTON

Washington, December 24, 1848

M Y DEAR FATHER:
Your letter of the 7th was received night before last. I very cheerfully send you the twenty dollars, which sum you say is necessary to save your land from sale. It is singular that you should have forgotten a judgment against you; and it is more singular that the plaintiff should have let you forget it so long, particularly as I

suppose you always had property enough to satisfy a judgment of that amount. Before you pay it, it would be well to be sure you have not paid, or at least that you cannot prove that you have paid it.

Give my love to mother and all the connections.

Affectionately your son,

A. LINCOLN

D EAR JOHNSTON:

Your request for eighty dollars I do not think it best to comply with now. At the various times when I have helped you a little you have said to me, "We can get along very well now;" but in a very short time I find you in the same difficulty again. Now, this can only happen by some defect in your conduct. What that defect is, I think I know. You are not lazy, and still you are an idler. I doubt whether, since I saw you, you have done a good whole day's work in any one day. You do not very much dislike to work, and still you do not work much, merely because it does not seem to you that you could get much for it. This habit of uselessly wasting time is the whole difficulty; it is vastly important to you, and still more so to your children, that you should break the habit. It is more important to them, because they have longer to live, and can keep out of an idle habit before they are in it, easier than they can get out after they are in.

You are now in need of some money; and what I propose is, that you shall go to work, "tooth and nail," for somebody who will give you money for it. Let father and your boys take charge of your things at home, prepare for a crop, and make a crop, and you go to work for the best money wages, or in discharge of any debt you owe, that you can get; and, to secure you a fair reward for your labor, I now promise you, that for every dollar you will, between this and the first of May, get for your own labor, either in money or as your own indebtedness, I will then give you one other dollar. By this, if you hire yourself at ten dollars a month, from me you will get ten more, making twenty dollars a month for your work. In this I do not mean you shall go off to St. Louis, or the lead mines, or the gold mines in California, but I mean for you to go at it for the best wages you can get close to home in Coles County. Now, if you will do this, you will be soon out of debt, and, what is better, you will have a habit that will keep you from getting in debt again. But, if I should now clear you out of debt, next year you would be just as deep in as ever. You say you would almost give your place in heaven for seventy or eighty dollars. Then you value your place in heaven very cheap, for I am sure you can, with the offer I make, get the seventy or eighty dollars for four or five months' work. You say if I will furnish you the money you will deed me the land, and, if you don't pay the money back, you will deliver possession. Nonsense! If you can't now live with the land, how will you then live without it? You have always been kind to me, and I do not mean to be unkind to you. On the contrary, if you will but follow my advice, you will find it worth more than eighty times eighty dollars to you.

Affectionately your brother,

A. LINCOLN

~~~~~~

"...smarter than he looks to be."

~~~~~~

A YOUNG *man by the name of Jonathan Birch, applying for admission to the bar, was given this note which said little but told much to Judge Logan, a co-member of the examining committee.*

LETTER TO JUDGE STEPHEN T. LOGAN

MY DEAR JUDGE—
The bearer of this is a young man who thinks he can be a lawyer. Examine him if you want to. I have done so and am satisfied. He's a good deal smarter than he looks to be.

Yours,

LINCOLN

~~~~~~

"I am not a very sentimental man. . . ."

~~~~~~

L̲ITTLE *suspecting that he would someday be besieged by autograph seekers, Lincoln couldn't understand why anyone should want his signature.*

LETTER TO C. U. SCHLATER

Washington, Jan. 5, 1849

MR. C. U. SCHLATER

D EAR SIR:
     Your note, requesting my 'signature with a sentiment' was received, and should have been answered long since, but that it was mislaid. I am not a very sentimental man; and the best sentiment I can think of is, that if you collect the signatures of all persons who are no less distinguished than I, you will have a very undistinguishing mass of names.

Yours respectfully,

A. LINCOLN

~~~~~~

"... and thank you to boot."

~~~~~~

IN *Lincoln's law dealings, his sense of fairness always pre-*
vailed over considerations of fee. What a surprised client
Abraham Bale must have been upon opening this note from
his lawyer.

LETTER TO ABRAHAM BALE

Springfield, Feb. 22, 1850

MR. ABRAHAM BALE,

DEAR SIR:
      I understand Mr. Hickox will go, or
send to Petersburg tomorrow, for the purpose of
meeting you to settle the difficulty about the
wheat. I sincerely hope you will settle it. I think
you *can* if you *will,* for I have always found Mr.
Hickox a fair man in his dealings. If you settle,
I will charge nothing for what I have done, and

thank you to boot. By settling, you will most likely get your money sooner and with much less trouble and expense.

Yours truly,

A. LINCOLN

~~~~~~

"if . . . you cannot be an honest lawyer,
resolve to be honest without being a lawyer."

~~~~~~

THIS *"Lawyer's Creed" was prepared by Lincoln for a con-*
templated lecture. The ideals expressed make it worthy of
inscription on the walls of every law office. That Lincoln
practiced what he preached is clearly indicated by many of
his letters in this collection.

NOTES FOR A LAW LECTURE

Circa July, 1850

I AM not an accomplished lawyer. I find quite
as much material for a lecture in those points
wherein I have failed, as in those wherein I have
been moderately successful. The leading rule for
the lawyer, as for the man of every other calling,
is diligence. Leave nothing for to-morrow which
can be done to-day. Never let your correspondence
fall behind. Whatever piece of business you have

in hand, before stopping, do all the labor pertaining to it which can then be done. When you bring a common-law suit, if you have the facts for doing so, write the declaration at once. If a law point be involved, examine the books, and note the authority you rely on upon the declaration itself, where you are sure to find it when wanted. The same of defenses and pleas. In business not likely to be litigated,—ordinary collection cases, foreclosures, partitions, and the like,—make all examinations of titles, and note them, and even draft orders and decrees in advance. This course has a triple advantage; it avoids omissions and neglect, saves your labor when once done, performs the labor out of court when you have leisure, rather than in court when you have not. Extemporaneous speaking should be practised and cultivated. It is the lawyer's avenue to the public. However able and faithful he may be in other respects, people are slow to bring him business if he cannot make a speech. And yet there is not a more fatal error to young lawyers than relying too much on speech-making. If any one, upon his rare powers of speaking, shall claim an exemption from the drudgery of the law, his case is a failure in advance.

Discourage litigation. Persuade your neighbors

to compromise whenever you can. Point out to them how the nominal winner is often a real loser —in fees, expenses, and waste of time. As a peacemaker the lawyer has a superior opportunity of being a good man. There will still be business enough.

Never stir up litigation. A worse man can scarcely be found than one who does this. Who can be more nearly a fiend than he who habitually overhauls the register of deeds in search of defects in titles, whereon to stir up strife, and put money in his pocket? A moral tone ought to be infused into the profession which should drive such men out of it.

The matter of fees is important, far beyond the mere question of bread and butter involved. Properly attended to, fuller justice is done to both lawyer and client. An exorbitant fee should never be claimed. As a general rule never take your whole fee in advance, nor any more than a small retainer. When fully paid beforehand, you are more than a common mortal if you can feel the same interest in the case, as if something was still in prospect for you, as well as for your client. And when you lack interest in the case the job will very likely lack skill and diligence in the performance. Settle the amount of fee and take a note in advance. Then you will feel that you are working for something, and you are sure to do your work faithfully and well. Never sell a fee note—at least not before the consideration service is performed. It leads to negligence and dishonesty—negligence by losing interest in the case, and dishonesty in refusing to refund when you have allowed the consideration to fail.

There is a vague popular belief that lawyers are necessarily dishonest. I say vague, because when we consider to what extent confidence and honors are reposed in and conferred upon lawyers by the people, it appears improbable that their impression of dishonesty is very distinct and vivid. Yet the impression is common, almost universal. Let no young man choosing the law for a calling for a moment yield to the popular belief—resolve to be honest at all events; and if in your own judgment you cannot be an honest lawyer, resolve to be honest without being a lawyer. Choose some other occupation, rather than one in the choosing of which you do, in advance, consent to be a knave.

~~~~~~

"Go to work is the only cure...."

~~~~~~

LINCOLN'S *anxiety for his step-mother, for whom he felt a deep affection, explains the harsh note which runs through this sound advice to his step-brother, John D. Johnston.*

LETTER TO JOHN D. JOHNSTON

Shelbyville, November 4, 1851

DEAR BROTHER:

When I came into Charleston day before yesterday, I learned that you are anxious to sell the land where you live and move to Missouri. I have been thinking of this ever since, and cannot but think such a notion is utterly foolish. What can you do in Missouri better than here? Is the land any richer? Can you there, any more than here, raise corn and wheat and oats without work? Will anybody there, any more than here, do your work for you? If you intend to go to work, there is no better place than right where you are;

if you do not intend to go to work, you cannot get along anywhere. Squirming and crawling about from place to place can do no good. You have raised no corn this year; and what you really want is to sell the land, get the money, and spend it. Part with the land you have, and, my life upon it, you will never after own a spot big enough to bury you in. Half you will get for the land you will spend in moving to Missouri, and the other half you will eat, drink, and wear out, and no foot of land will be bought. Now, I feel it my duty to have no hand in such a piece of foolery. I feel that it is so even on your own account, and particularly on mother's account. The eastern forty acres I intend to keep for mother while she lives; if you will not cultivate it, it will rent for enough to support her—at least, it will rent for something. Her dower in the other two forties she can let you have, and no thanks to me. Now, do not misunderstand this letter; I do not write it in any unkindness. I write it in order, if possible, to get you to face the truth, which truth is, you are destitute because you have idled away all your time. Your thousand pretenses for not getting along better are all nonsense; they deceive nobody but yourself. Go to work is the only cure for your case.

A. LINCOLN

"... poor and a cripple as he is...."

Lincoln *explains to a client why he has not taken judgment for him against a poor cripple.*

LETTER TO L. M. HAYS

Springfield, Oct. 27, 1852

L. M. HAYS, Esq.

Dear Sir:
Yours of Sept. 30th just received. At our court, just passed, I could have got a judgment against Turley, if I had pressed to the utmost; but I am really sorry for him—*poor,* and a *cripple* as he is— He begged time to try to find evidence to prove that the deceased on his death bed, ordered the note to be given up to him or destroyed. I do not suppose he will get any such evidence, but I allowed him until next court to try.

Yours &c

A. Lincoln

[35]

~~~~~~

"Most governments have been based on the denial of equal rights of men. . . ."

~~~~~~

AMONG *the many papers assiduously preserved by his secretaries Nicolay and Hay is this fragment in Lincoln's handwriting summing up his early views on slavery.*

FRAGMENT

Circa **July, 1854**

THE ant who has toiled and dragged a crumb to his nest will furiously defend the fruit of his labor against whatever robber assails him. So plain that the most dumb and stupid slave that ever toiled for a master does constantly know that he is wronged. So plain that no one, high or low, ever does mistake it, except in a plainly selfish way; for although volume upon volume is written to prove slavery a very good thing, we never hear of the man who wishes to take the good of it by being a slave himself.

Most governments have been based, practically, on the denial of the equal rights of men, as I have, in part, stated them; ours began by affirming those rights. They said, some men are too ignorant and vicious to share in government. Possibly so, said we; and, by your system, you would always keep them ignorant and vicious. We proposed to give all a chance; and we expected the weak to grow stronger, the ignorant wiser, and all better and happier together.

We made the experiment, and the fruit is before us. Look at it, think of it. Look at it in its aggregate grandeur, of extent of country, and numbers of population—of ship, and steamboat, and railroad.

"I have really got it into my head. . . ."

LINCOLN *"takes it into his head"* to run for the Senate but first makes sure to win the support of an influential friend and potential rival.

LETTER TO JOSEPH GILLESPIE

Springfield, December 1, 1854

MY DEAR SIR:

I have really got it into my head to try to be United States Senator, and, if I could have your support, my chances would be reasonably good. But I know, and acknowledge, that you have as just claims to the place as I have; and therefore I cannot ask you to yield to me, if you are thinking of becoming a candidate, yourself. If, however, you are not, then I should like to be remembered affectionately by you; and also to have you make a mark for me with the Anti-Nebraska members, down your way.

If you know, and have no objection to tell, let me know whether Trumbull intends to make a push. If he does, I suppose the two men in St. Clair, and one, or both, in Madison, will be for him. We have the legislature, clearly enough, on joint ballot, but the Senate is very close, and Cullom told me to-day that the Nebraska men will stave off the election, if they can. Even if we get into joint vote, we shall have difficulty to unite our forces. Please write me, and let this be confidential.

Your friend as ever,

A. LINCOLN

"...I am not Senator."

LINCOLN announces that he has thrown his senatorial votes to Trumbull to further the cause of the Party.

LETTER TO W. H. HENDERSON

Springfield, Ill., Feb. 21, 1855

HON. W. H. HENDERSON

MY DEAR SIR:

The election is over, the session is ended and I am not Senator. I have to content myself with the honor of having been the first choice of a large majority of the fifty-one members who finally made the election. My larger number of friends had to surrender to Trumbull's smaller number, in order to prevent the election of Matteson, which would have been a Douglas victory. I started with 44 votes and T. with 5. It is rather hard for the 44 to have to surrender to the 5 and a less good humored man than I, perhaps, would not have consented to it,—and it would not have been done without my consent. I could not, however, let the whole political result go to smash, on a point merely personal to myself.

Yours, etc.

A. LINCOLN

~~~~~~

"If for this you and I must differ, differ we must."

~~~~~~

KNOWING *full well that this letter would severely test his long-time friendship with Josh Speed, Lincoln completely unburdens himself on the question of slavery and individual liberty.*

LETTER TO JOSHUA F. SPEED

Springfield, August 24, 1855

DEAR SPEED:

You know what a poor correspondent I am. Ever since I received your very agreeable letter of the 22d of May I have been intending to write you an answer to it. You suggest that in political action, now, you and I would differ. I suppose we would; not quite as much, however, as you may think. You know I dislike slavery, and you fully admit the abstract wrong of it. So far there is no cause of difference. But you say that sooner than yield your legal right to the slave, especially at the bidding of those who are not themselves interested, you would see the Union dissolved. I am not aware that any one is bidding you yield that right; very certainly I am not. I leave that matter entirely to yourself. I also acknowledge your rights and my obligations under the Constitution in regard to your slaves. I confess I hate to see the poor creatures hunted down and caught and carried back to their stripes and un-requited toil; but I bite my lips and keep quiet. In 1841 you and I had together a tedious low-water trip on a steamboat from Louisville to St. Louis. You may remember, as I well do, that from Louisville to the mouth of the Ohio there were on board ten or a dozen slaves shackled together with irons. That sight was a continued torment to me, and I see something like it every time I touch the Ohio or any other slave border. It is not fair for you to assume that I have no interest in a thing which has, and continually exercises, the power of making me miserable. You ought rather to appreciate how much the great body of the Northern people do crucify their feelings, in order to maintain their loyalty to the Constitution and the Union. I do oppose the extension of slavery because my judgment and feeling so prompt me, and I am under no obligations to the contrary. If for this you and I must differ, differ we must. You say, if you were President, you would send an army and hang the leaders of the Missouri outrages upon the Kansas elections; still, if Kansas fairly votes herself a slave State she must be admitted, or the Union must be dissolved. But how if she votes herself a slave State unfairly, that is, by the very means for which you say you would hang men? Must she still be admitted, or the Union dissolved? That will be the phase of the question when it first becomes a practical one. In your assumption that there may be a fair decision of the slavery question in Kansas, I plainly see you and I would differ about the Nebraska law. I look upon that enactment not as a law, but as a violence from the beginning. It was conceived in violence, is maintained in violence, and is being executed in violence. I say it was conceived in violence, because the destruction of the Missouri Compromise, under the circumstances, was nothing less than violence. It was passed in violence, because it could not have passed at all but for the votes of many members in violence of the known will of their constituents. It is maintained in violence, because the elections since clearly demand its repeal; and the demand is openly disregarded.

You say men ought to be hung for the way they are executing the law; I say the way it is being executed is quite as good as any of its antecedents. It is being executed in the precise way which was intended from the first, else why does no Nebraska man express astonishment or condemnation? Poor Reeder is the only public man who has been silly enough to believe that anything like fairness was ever intended, and he has been bravely undeceived.

That Kansas will form a slave constitution, and with it will ask to be admitted into the Union, I take to be already a settled question, and so settled by the very means you so pointedly condemn. By every principle of law ever held by any court North or South, every negro taken to Kansas is free; yet, in utter disregard of this,—in the spirit of violence merely,—that beautiful legislature gravely passes a law to hang any man who shall venture to inform a negro of his legal rights. This is the subject and real object of the law. If, like Haman, they should hang upon the gallows of their own building, I shall not be among the mourners for their fate. In my humble sphere, I shall advocate the restoration of the Missouri Compromise so long as Kansas remains a Territory, and when, by all these foul means, it seeks to come into the Union as a slave State, I shall oppose it. I am very loath in any case to withhold my assent to the enjoyment of property acquired or located in good faith; but I do not admit that good faith in taking a negro to Kansas to be held in slavery is a probability with any man. Any man who has sense enough to be the controller of his own property has too much sense to misunderstand the outrageous character of the whole Nebraska business. But I digress. In my opposition to the admission of Kansas I shall have some company, but we may be beaten. If we are, I shall not on that account attempt to dissolve the Union. I think it probable, however, we shall be beaten. Standing as a unit among yourselves, you can, directly and indirectly, bribe enough of our men to carry the day, as you could on the open proposition to establish a monarchy. Get hold of some man in the North whose position and ability is such that he can make the support of your measure, whatever it may be, a Democratic party necessity, and the thing is done. Apropos of this, let me tell you an anecdote. Douglas introduced the

Nebraska bill in January. In February afterward there was a called session of the Illinois legislature. Of the one hundred members composing the two branches of that body, about seventy were Democrats. These latter held a caucus, in which the Nebraska bill was talked of, if not formally discussed. It was thereby discovered that just three, and no more, were in favor of the measure. In a day or two Douglas's orders came on to have resolutions passed approving the bill; and they were passed by large majorities!!! The truth of this is vouched for by a bolting Democratic member. The masses, too, Democratic as well as Whig, were even nearer unanimous against it; but, as soon as the party necessity of supporting it became apparent, the way the Democrats began to see the wisdom and justice of it was perfectly astonishing.

You say that if Kansas fairly votes herself a free State, as a Christian you will rejoice at it. All decent slaveholders talk that way, and I do not doubt their candor. But they never vote that way. Although in a private letter or conversation you will express your preference that Kansas shall be free, you would vote for no man for Congress who would say the same thing publicly. No such man could be elected from any district in a slave State.

You think Stringfellow and company ought to be hung; and yet at the next presidential election you will vote for the exact type and representative of Stringfellow. The slave-breeders and slave-traders are a small, odious, and detested class among you; and yet in politics they dictate the course of all of you, and are as completely your masters as you are the master of your own negroes. You inquire where I now stand. That is a disputed point. I think I am a Whig; but others say there are no Whigs, and that I am an Abolitionist. When I was at Washington, I voted for the Wilmot proviso as good as forty times; and I never heard of any one attempting to unwhig me for that. I now do no more than oppose the extension of slavery. I am not a Know-nothing; that is certain. How could I be? How can any one who abhors the oppression of negroes be in favor of degrading classes of white people? Our progress in degeneracy appears to me to be pretty rapid. As a nation we began by declaring that "all men are created equal." We now practically read it "all men are created equal, except negroes." When the Know-nothings get control, it will read "all men are created equal, except negroes and foreigners and Catholics." When it comes to this,

I shall prefer emigrating to some country where they make no pretense of loving liberty,—to Russia, for instance, where despotism can be taken pure, and without the base alloy of hypocrisy.

Mary will probably pass a day or two in Louisville in October. My kindest regards to Mrs. Speed. On the leading subject of this letter, I have more of her sympathy than I have of yours; and yet let me say I am

Your friend forever,

A. LINCOLN

~~~~~~

"Here's your old chalked hat."

~~~~~~

IN *the backwoods jargon that characterizes much of his hardy humor, Lincoln asks for a new railroad pass from the superintendent of the Alton.*

LETTER TO R. P. MORGAN

Springfield, February 13, 1856

DEAR SIR:

Says Tom to John: "Here's your old rotten wheelbarrow. I've broke it, usin' on it. I wish you would mend it, case I shall want to borrow it this arter-noon."

Acting on this as a precedent, I say, "Here's your old, chalked hat.' I wish you would take it, and send me a new one; case I shall want to use it the first of March."

Yours truly,

A. LINCOLN

"You must think I am a high-priced man."

THIS *letter typifies the many acts that earned for its writer the sobriquet "Honest Abe."*

LETTER TO GEORGE P. FLOYD

Springfield, Illinois, February 21, 1856

MR. GEORGE P. FLOYD,
QUINCY, ILLINOIS

DEAR SIR:
        I have just received yours of 16th, with check on Flagg & Savage for twenty-five dollars. You must think I am a high-priced man. You are too liberal with your money.

Fifteen dollars is enough for the job. I send you a receipt for fifteen dollars, and return to you a ten-dollar bill.

Yours truly,

A. LINCOLN

[51]

~~~~~~

"...I argued your case better than my own. ..."

~~~~~~

WHEN *a young lawyer who opposed him lacked sufficient funds to stay a week in Springfield until the case came up, Lincoln volunteered to argue both sides before the Supreme Court. In this letter Lincoln announces the judges' decision to his absent adversary.*

LETTER TO HENRY WALKER BISHOP

MY DEAR MR. BISHOP:
The Supreme Court came in on the appointed day and I did my best to keep faith with you. Apparently I argued your case better than my own, for the court has just sent down a rescript in your favor. Accept my heartiest congratulations.

Very sincerely yours,

A. LINCOLN

~~~~~~

"... my running would hurt and not help the cause."

~~~~~~

IN *the year The Republican Party was formed Lincoln worked hard for its success, but declined when the President of Illinois College suggested that he himself be the young party's candidate for Congress.*

LETTER TO JULIAN M. STURTEVANT

Springfield, Sept. 27, 1856

MY DEAR SIR:
Owing to absence yours of the 16th, was not received until the day before yesterday. I thank you for your good opinion of me personally, and still more for the deep interest you take in the cause of our common country. It pains me a little that you have deemed it necessary to point out to me how I may be compensated for throwing myself in the breach now. This assumes that

I am merely calculating the chances of personal advancement. Let me assure you that I decline to be a candidate for congress, on my clear conviction that my running would hurt and not help the cause. I am willing to make any personal sacrifice, but I am not willing to do, what in my own judgment, is a sacrifice of the cause itself.

Very truly yours,

A. LINCOLN

Lincoln's Challenge to Douglas

WHEN *Lincoln first determined to pose to Stephen Douglas the question of the legality of slavery in the Territories, his friends warned him that he would lose the election. "Gentlemen," said Lincoln, "I am killing larger game; if Douglas answers, he can never be President, and the battle of 1860 is worth a hundred of this." In these simple terms Lincoln proposed the historic debates:*

TO STEPHEN A. DOUGLAS

Chicago, Illinois, July 24, 1858

MY DEAR SIR:

Will it be agreeable to you to make an arrangement for you and myself to divide time, and address the same audiences the present canvass? Mr. Judd, who will hand you this, is authorized to receive your answer; and, if agreeable to you, to enter into the terms of such arrangement.

Your obedient servant,

A. LINCOLN

"... I accede. ..."

IN *equally simple words Lincoln accepted Douglas's terms, choosing to waive but not to overlook the advantage "The Little Giant" had taken.*

TO STEPHEN A. DOUGLAS

Springfield, July 31, 1858

DEAR SIR:
Yours of yesterday, naming places, times, and terms for joint discussions between us, was received this morning. Although by the terms, as you propose, you take four openings and closes to my three, I accede, and thus close the arrangement. I direct this to you at Hillsboro, and shall try to have both your letter and this appear in the "Journal" and "Register" of Monday morning.

Your obedient servant,

A. LINCOLN

"And this too shall pass away."

*I*N *one of his speeches Lincoln alludes to the Eastern monarch who once charged his wise men to invent him a sentence to be ever in view, and which would be true and appropriate in all times and situations. They presented him the words, "And this, too, shall pass away." Lincoln found this quotation particularly apt in writing to the Republican State Chairman, after the unsuccessful election of 1858.*

LETTER TO N. B. JUDD

Springfield, November 16, 1858

D EAR SIR:
Yours of the 15th is just received. I wrote you the same day. As to the pecuniary matter, I am willing to pay according to my ability; but I am the poorest hand living to get others to pay.

I have been on expenses so long without earning anything that I am absolutely without money now for even household purposes. Still, if you can put in two hundred and fifty dollars for me toward discharging the debt of the committee, I will allow it when you and I settle the private matter between us.

This, with what I have already paid, and with an outstanding note of mine, will exceed my subscription of five hundred dollars. This, too, is exclusive of my ordinary expenses during the campaign, all of which being added to my loss of time and business, bears pretty heavily upon one no better off in [this] world's goods than I; but as I had the post of honor, it is not for me to be over nice. You are feeling badly,—"And this too shall pass away," never fear.

Yours as ever,

A. Lincoln

"The cause of civil liberty must not be surrendered. . . ."

LINCOLN *lost the election to Douglas as his friends had predicted, but never wavered from his conviction that right would prevail.*

LETTER TO HENRY ASBURY

Springfield, November 19, 1858

DEAR SIR:

Yours of the 13th was received some days ago. The fight must go on. The cause of civil liberty must not be surrendered at the end of one or even one hundred defeats. Douglas had the ingenuity to be supported in the late contest both as the best means to break down and to uphold the slave interest. No ingenuity can keep these antagonistic elements in harmony long. Another explosion will soon come.

Yours truly,

A. LINCOLN

THE *essence of democracy, as Lincoln saw it, was succinctly expressed in his own handwriting in the form of an autograph.*

LINCOLN AUTOGRAPH

AS I would not be a *slave,* so I would not be a *master.* This expresses my idea of democracy. Whatever differs from this, to the extent of the difference, is no democracy.

A. LINCOLN

As I would not be a slave, so I would not be a master. This expresses my idea of democracy — Whatever differs from this, to the extent of the difference, is no democracy —

A. Lincoln —

~~~~~~

"The principles of Jefferson. . . ."

~~~~~~

Because *of the simple majesty of its phrase, this is one of Lincoln's most distinguished letters. It was written to a committee who had invited him to attend a celebration of the birthday of Thomas Jefferson.*

LETTER TO H. L. PIERCE & OTHERS

Springfield, Ill., April 6, 1859

Gentlemen:

Your kind note inviting me to attend a festival in Boston, on the 28th instant, in honor of the birthday of Thomas Jefferson, was duly received. My engagements are such that I cannot attend.

Bearing in mind that about seventy years ago two great political parties were first formed in this country, that Thomas Jefferson was the head of one of them and Boston the headquarters of the other, it is both curious and interesting that those supposed to descend politically from the party opposed to Jefferson should now be celebrating his birthday in their own original seat of empire, while those claiming political descent from him have nearly ceased to breathe his name everywhere.

Remembering, too, that the Jefferson party was formed upon its supposed superior devotion to the personal rights of men, holding the rights of property to be secondary only, and greatly inferior, and assuming that the so-called Democracy of to-day are the Jefferson, and their opponents the anti-Jefferson, party, it will be equally interesting to note how completely the two have changed hands as to the principle upon which they were originally supposed to be divided. The Democracy of to-day hold the liberty of one man to be absolutely nothing, when in conflict with another man's right of property; Republicans, on the contrary, are for both the man and the dollar, but in case of conflict the man before the dollar.

I remember being once much amused at seeing two partially intoxicated men engaged in a fight with their great-coats on, which fight, after a long and rather harmless contest, ended in each having fought himself out of his own coat and into that of the other. If the two leading parties of this day are really identical with the two in the days of Jefferson and Adams, they have performed the same feat as the two drunken men.

But, soberly, it is now no child's play to save the principles of Jefferson from total overthrow in this nation. One would state with great confidence that he could convince any sane child that the simpler propositions of Euclid are true; but nevertheless he would fail, utterly, with one who should deny the definitions and axioms. The principles of Jefferson are the definitions and axioms of free society. And yet they are denied and evaded, with no small show of success. One dashingly calls them "glittering generalities." Another bluntly calls them "self-evident lies." And others insidiously argue that they apply to "superior races." These expressions, differing in form, are identical in object and effect—the supplanting of the principles of free government, and restoring those of classification, caste, and legitimacy. They would delight a convocation of crowned heads plotting against the people. They are the vanguard, the miners and sappers of returning despotism. We must repulse them, or they will subjugate us. This is a world of compensation; and he who would be no slave must consent to have no slave. Those who deny freedom to others deserve it not for themselves, and, under a just God, cannot long retain it. All honor to Jefferson—to the man, who, in the concrete pressure of a struggle for national independence by a single people, had the coolness, forecast, and capacity to introduce into a merely revolutionary document an abstract truth, applicable to all men and all times, and so to embalm it there that to-day and in all coming days it shall be a rebuke and a stumbling-block to the very harbingers of reappearing tyranny and oppression.

Your obedient servant,

A. LINCOLN

~~~~~~

"...a large rat-hole...."

~~~~~~

BELIEVING *material possessions to be a poor measure of a man's true mettle, Lincoln had little patience with a New York firm that wrote inquiring about a man he knew in Springfield.*

LETTER TO NEW YORK FIRM

YOURS OF THE 10TH RECEIVED. First of all, he has a wife and a baby; together they ought to be worth $500,000 to any man. Secondly, he has an office in which there is a table worth $1.50 and three chairs worth, say, $1. Last of all, there is in one corner a large rat-hole, which will bear looking into.

Respectfully,

A. LINCOLN

~~~~~~

"... I do not think myself fit for the presidency."

~~~~~~

To the editor of a Rock Island newspaper, who wished to start a "Lincoln for President" boom, "Humble Abe" expressed his appreciation and, at the same time, his feeling of inadequacy. This was selected by John G. Nicolay as one of three letters most representative of Lincoln at his best.

LETTER TO T. J. PICKETT

Springfield, April 16, 1859

MY DEAR SIR:
Yours of the 13th is just received. My engagements are such that I cannot at any very early day visit Rock Island to deliver a lecture, or for any other object. As to the other matter you kindly mention, I must in candor say I do not think myself fit for the presidency. I certainly am flattered and gratified that some partial friends think of me in that connection; but I really think

it best for our cause that no concerted effort, such as you suggest, should be made. Let this be considered confidential.

Yours very truly,

A. LINCOLN

"... in regard to naturalized citizens. ..."

REPLYING *to the editor of one of the largest German newspapers, Lincoln declares himself upon the "anti-alien" issue in words that cannot be misunderstood.*

LETTER TO DR. THEODORE CANISIUS

Springfield, May 17, 1859

DEAR SIR:

Your note asking, in behalf of yourself and other German citizens, whether I am for or against the constitutional provision in regard to naturalized citizens, lately adopted by Massachusetts, and whether I am for or against a fusion of the Republicans, and other opposition elements, for the canvass of 1860, is received.

Massachusetts is a sovereign and independent State; and it is no privilege of mine to scold her for what she does. Still, if from what she has done an inference is sought to be drawn as to what I would do, I may without impropriety speak out. I say, then, that, as I understand the Massachusetts provision, I am against its adoption in Illinois, or in any other place where I have a right to oppose it. Understanding the spirit of our institutions to aim at the elevation of men, I am opposed to whatever tends to degrade them. I have some little notoriety for commiserating the oppressed negro; and I should be strangely inconsistent if I could favor any project for curtailing the existing rights of white men, even though born in different lands, and speaking different languages from myself. As to the matter of fusion, I am for it, if it can be had on Republican grounds; and I am not for it on any other terms. A fusion on any other terms would be as foolish as unprincipled. It would lose the whole North, while the common enemy would still carry the whole South. The question of men is a different one. There are good patriotic men and able statesmen in the South whom I would cheerfully support, if they would now place themselves on Republican ground, but I am against letting down the Republican standard a hair's-breadth.

I have written this hastily, but I believe it answers your questions substantially.

Yours truly,

A. LINCOLN

~~~~~~

Lincoln's Sketch of His Life

~~~~~~

HIDING *his modesty behind a screen of humor, Lincoln pens a two-page sketch of his life for his friend and ardent booster, J. W. Fell.*

LETTER TO J. W. FELL

Springfield, December 20, 1859

MY DEAR SIR:
Herewith is a little sketch, as you requested. There is not much of it, for the reason, I suppose, that there is not much of me. If anything be made out of it, I wish it to be modest, and not to go beyond the material. If it were thought necessary to incorporate anything from any of my speeches, I suppose there would be no objection. Of course it must not appear to have been written by myself.

Yours very truly,

A. LINCOLN

I was born February 12, 1809, in Hardin County, Kentucky. My parents were both born in Virginia, of undistinguished families—second families, perhaps I should say. My mother, who died in my tenth year, was of a family of the name of Hanks, some of whom now reside in Adams, and others in Macon County, Illinois. My paternal grandfather, Abraham Lincoln, emigrated from Rockingham County, Virginia, to Kentucky about 1781 or 1782, where a year or two later he was killed by the Indians, not in battle, but by stealth, when he was laboring to open a farm in the forest. His ancestors, who were Quakers, went to Virginia from Berks County, Pennsylvania. An effort to identify them with the New England family of the same name ended in nothing more definite than a similarity of Christian names in both families, such as Enoch, Levi, Mordecai, Solomon, Abraham, and the like.

My father, at the death of his father, was but six years of age, and he grew up literally without education. He removed from Kentucky to what is now Spencer County, Indiana, in my eighth year. We reached our new home about the time the State came into the Union. It was a wild region, with many bears and other wild animals still in the woods. There I grew up. There were some schools, so called, but no qualification was ever required of a teacher beyond "readin', writin', and cipherin'" to the rule of three. If a straggler supposed to understand Latin happened to sojourn in the neighborhood, he was looked upon as a wizard. There was absolutely nothing to excite ambition for education. Of course, when I came of age I did not know much. Still, somehow, I could read, write, and cipher to the rule of three, but that was all. I have not been to school since. The little advance I now have upon this store of education, I have picked up from time to time under the pressure of necessity.

I was raised to farm work, which I continued till I was twenty-two. At twenty-one I came to Illinois, Macon County. Then I got to New Salem, at that time in Sangamon, now in Menard County, where I remained a year as a sort of clerk in a store. Then came the Black Hawk war; and I was elected a captain of volunteers, a success which gave me more pleasure than any I have had since. I went the campaign, was elated, ran for the legislature the same year (1832), and was beaten—the only time I ever have been beaten by the people. The next and three succeeding biennial elections I was elected to the legislature. I was not a candidate afterward. During this legislative period I had studied law, and removed to Springfield to practise it. In 1846 I was once elected to the lower House of Congress. Was not a candidate for reelection. From 1849 to 1854, both inclusive, practised law more assiduously than ever before. Always a Whig in politics; and generally on the Whig electoral tickets, making active canvasses. I was losing interest in politics when the repeal of the Missouri compromise aroused me again. What I have done since then is pretty well known.

If any personal description of me is thought desirable, it may be said I am, in height, six feet four inches, nearly; lean in flesh, weighing on an average one hundred and eighty pounds; dark complexion, with coarse black hair and gray eyes. No other marks or brands recollected.

Yours truly,

A. LINCOLN

~~~~~~

"A house divided against itself cannot stand."

~~~~~~

L INCOLN'S *famous "House Divided Speech" placed him squarely in the middle of a raging national controversy. Many persons, including Douglas, sought to discredit him by placing upon his words interpretations which he had never intended. Lincoln replied to this heckling by plainly stating, "I meant all I said, and did not mean anything I did not say."*

LETTER TO
O. P. HALL, J. R. FULLENWIDER &
U. F. CORRELL

Springfield, Feb. 14, 1860

MESSRS. O. P. HALL,
J. R. FULLENWIDER &
U. F. CORRELL

G ENTLEMEN:
Your letter in which, among other things, you ask what I meant when I said this

"Union could not stand half slave and half free"; and also what I meant when I said "a house divided against itself could not stand" is received and I very cheerfully answer it as plainly as I may be able. You misquote, to some material extent, what I did say, which induces me to think you have not very carefully read the speech in which the expressions occur which puzzle you to understand. For this reason and because the language I used is as plain as I can make it, I now quote at length the whole paragraph in which the expressions which puzzle you occur. It is as follows: "We are now far into the fifth year since a policy was initiated with the avowed object and confident promise of putting an end to slavery agitation. Under the operation of that policy that agitation has not only not ceased, but constantly augmented. I believe it will not cease until a crisis shall have been reached, and passed. A house divided against itself can not stand. I believe this government can not endure *permanently*, half slave, and half free. I do not expect the Union to be dissolved: I do not expect the house to fall; but I do expect it will cease to be divided. It will become all one thing, or all the other. Either the opponents of slavery will avert the further spread of it and place it where the public mind shall rest in the belief that it is in course of ultimate extinction; or its advocates will push it forward till it will become alike lawful in all the states, old as well as new, North as well as South."

That is the whole paragraph; and it puzzles me to make my meaning plainer. Look over it carefully, and conclude I meant all I said, and did not mean any thing I did not say, and you will have my meaning. Douglas attacked me upon this, saying it was a declaration of war between the slave and the free states. You will perceive, I said no such thing, and I assure you I thought of no such thing. If I had said I believe the Government cannot last always half slave and half free, would you understand it any better than you do? Endure permanently and last always have exactly the same meaning. If you, or [*sic*] if you will state to me some meaning which you suppose I had, I can and will instantly tell you whether that was my meaning.

Yours very truly,

A. Lincoln

*". . . painfully sensible of the great
responsibility. . . ."*

FINDING *it difficult to realize that he has been singled
out for the highest position in the nation, Lincoln replies to
the committee sent by the Chicago Convention notifying him
of his nomination.*

REPLY TO CHICAGO CONVENTION
COMMITTEE

Springfield, Illinois, May 21, 1860

MR. CHAIRMAN AND GENTLEMEN
OF THE COMMITTEE:
I tender to you, and through you to
the Republican National Convention, and all the
people represented in it, my profoundest thanks
for the high honor done me, which you now formally announce.

Deeply and even painfully sensible of the great

[77]

responsibility which is inseparable from this high honor—a responsibility which I could almost wish had fallen upon some one of the far more eminent men and experienced statesmen whose distinguished names were before the convention—I shall, by your leave, consider more fully the resolutions of the convention, denominated [in] the platform, and without any unnecessary or unreasonable delay respond to you, Mr. Chairman, in writing, not doubting that the platform will be found satisfactory, and the nomination gratefully accepted.

And now I will not longer defer the pleasure of taking you, and each of you, by the hand.

~~~~~~

Cooper Institute Speech

~~~~~~

CHARLES NOTT, *writing on behalf of The Young Men's Republican Union and wishing to publish Lincoln's already famous speech delivered at The Cooper Institute, suggested certain changes to make it "as nearly perfect as may be." Lincoln's reply reveals many secrets of his style and lends proof to Nott's own observation that "like a good arch—moving one word tumbles a whole sentence down."*

LETTER TO CHARLES C. NOTT

Springfield, Ills., May 31, 1860

CHARLES C. NOTT, ESQ.

MY DEAR SIR:

Yours of the 23rd, accompanied by a copy of the speech delivered by me at the Cooper Institute, and upon which you have made some notes for emendations, was received some days ago. Of course I would not object to, but would be pleased rather, with a more perfect edition of that speech.

I did not preserve memoranda of my investigations; and I could not now re-examine, and make notes, without an expenditure of time which I can not bestow upon it. Some of your notes I do not understand.

So far as it is intended merely to improve in grammar and elegance of composition, I am quite agreed; but I do not wish the sense changed, or modified, to a hair's breadth. And you, not having studied the particular points so closely as I have, can not be quite sure that you do not change the sense when you do not intend it. For instance, in a note at bottom of first page, you propose to substitute "Democrats" for "Douglas." But what I am saying there is *true* of Douglas, and is not true of "Democrats" generally; so that the proposed substitution would be a very considerable blunder. Your proposed insertion of "residences" though it would do little or no harm, is not at all necessary to the sense I was trying to convey. On page 5 your proposed grammatical change would certainly do no harm. The *"impudently absurd"* I stick to. The striking out "he" and inserting "we" turns the sense exactly wrong. The striking out "upon it" leaves the sense too general and incomplete. The sense is "act as they acted *upon that question*"—not as they acted generally.

After considering your proposed changes on page 7, I do not think them material, but I am willing to defer to you in relation to them.

On page 9, striking out "to us" is probably right. The word "lawyer's" I wish retained. The word "Courts" struck out twice, I wish reduced to "Court" and retained. "Court" as a collective noun properly governs the plural "have" as I understand. "The" preceding "Court," in the latter case, must also be retained. The words "quite," "as," and "or" on the same page, I wish retained. The italicising, and quotation marking, I have no objection to.

As to the note at bottom, I do not think any too much is admitted. What you propose on page 11, is right. I return your copy of the speech, together with one printed here, under my own hasty supervising. That at New York was printed without any supervision by me. If you conclude to publish a new edition, allow me to see the proof-sheets.

And now thanking you for your very complimentary letter, and your interest for me generally, I subscribe myself.

Your friend and servant,

A. Lincoln

"Abraham" or "Abram"

In this letter to the Republican Chairman, Lincoln concludes that the spelling of his first name really doesn't make much difference.

LETTER TO GEORGE ASHMUN

Springfield, Illinois, June 4, 1860

MY DEAR SIR:
It seems as if the question whether my first name is "Abraham" or "Abram" will never be settled. It is "Abraham," and if the letter of acceptance is not yet in print, you may, if you think fit, have my signature thereto printed "Abraham Lincoln." Exercise your judgment about this.

Yours as ever,

A. LINCOLN

" 'Must' is the word."

LINCOLN, *who knew only too well the need for persever-ance, sends a few words of advice and encouragement to a friend of his son who failed to enter Harvard.*

LETTER TO GEORGE LATHAM

Springfield, Ills., July 22, 1860

MY DEAR GEORGE:

I have scarcely felt greater pain in my life than on learning yesterday from Bob's letter, that you had failed to enter Harvard University. And yet there is very little in it, if you will allow no feeling of *discouragement* to seize, and prey upon you. It is a *certain* truth, that you *can* enter, and graduate in, Harvard University; and having made the attempt, you *must* succeed in it. *'Must'* is the word.

I know not how to aid you, save in the assur-

[83]

ance of one of mature age, and much severe experience, that you *can* not fail, if you resolutely determine that you *will* not.

The President of the institution, can scarcely be other than a kind man; and doubtless he would grant you an interview, and point out the readiest way to remove, or overcome, the obstacles which have thwarted you.

In your temporary failure there is no evidence that you may not yet be a better scholar, and a more successful man in the great struggle of life, than many others, who have entered College more easily.

Again I say let no feeling of discouragement prey upon you, and in the end you are sure to succeed.

With more than a common interest I subscribe myself

Very truly your friend,

A. Lincoln

~~~~~~

"...the 'soap question'...."

~~~~~~

Wнем *a Professor Gardner applied to the President-Elect for a soap testimonial, he good-humoredly complied, quoting his "superior officer" in domestic affairs.*

LETTER TO PROFESSOR GARDNER

Springfield, Ill., September 28, 1860

Dear SIR:

Some specimens of your Soap have been used at our house and Mrs. L. declares it is a superior article. She at the same time protests that *I* have never given sufficient attention to the "soap question" to be a competent judge.

Yours very truly,

A. Lincoln

THOMAS MADIGAN, *the famous dealer in Lincoln manu-scripts, considered this one of the sixteenth President's most characteristic letters, both in sentiment and phraseology.*

LETTER TO WILLIAM D. KELLY

Private.

Springfield, Ills., Oct, 13, 1860

HON. WILLIAM D. KELLY.

MY DEAR SIR:
Yours of the 6th asking permission to inscribe your new legal work to me, is received. Gratefully accepting the proffered honor, I give the leave, begging only that the inscription may be in modest terms, not representing me as a man of great learning, or a very extraordinary one in any respect.

Yours very truly,

A. LINCOLN

Private

Springfield, Ills. Oct. 13. 1860

Hon. William D. Kelly
My dear Sir:
Yours of the 6th.
asking permission to inscribe your
new legal work to me, is received.
Gratefully accepting the proffered
honor, I give the leave, begging only
that the inscription may be in modest
terms, not representing me as a man
of great learning, or a very extraordinary one in any respect—
Yours very truly
A. Lincoln.

A characteristically modest letter, only recently
brought to light, and not included in any of the
standard Lincoln collections.

Facsimile reproduction of Lincoln's famed "whiskers" letter to little Grace Bedell.

"As to the whiskers. . . ."

A LITTLE *girl of Westfield, New York, wrote Mr. Lincoln: "I am a little girl, eleven years old. . . . have you any little girls about as large as I am. . . . if you will let your whiskers grow. . . . you would look a great deal better for your face is so thin. . . . I must not write any more answer this right off. Good Bye." Grace Bedell.*

LETTER TO GRACE BEDELL

Springfield, Illinois, October 19, 1860

MY DEAR LITTLE MISS:
Your very agreeable letter of the 15th is received. I regret the necessity of saying I have no daughter. I have three sons—one seventeen, one nine, and one seven years of age. They, with their mother, constitute my whole family. As to the whiskers, having never worn any, do you not think

people would call it a piece of silly affectation if I were to begin it now?

Your very sincere well-wisher,

A. LINCOLN

Not long afterwards, Lincoln let his beard grow. Happening to pass through Westfield, he asked for his little friend and said, "You see I let these whiskers grow for you, Grace."

"If they hear not Moses. . . ."

LINCOLN, *having many times declared his intentions to prevent the spread of slavery to the Territories and not to interfere with slavery in the States, sees no possible good in restating his position to those who will not "read or heed."*

LETTER TO WILLIAM S. SPEER

(Confidential)

Springfield, Illinois, October 23, 1860

MY DEAR SIR:
Yours of the 13th was duly received. I appreciate your motive when you suggest the propriety of my writing for the public something disclaiming all intention to interfere with slaves or slavery in the States; but in my judgment it would do no good. I have already done this many, many times; and it is in print, and open to all who will read. Those who will not read or heed

what I have already publicly said would not read
or heed a repetition of it. "If they hear not Moses
and the prophets, neither will they be persuaded
though one rose from the dead."

Yours truly,

A. LINCOLN

"That, I suppose is the rub."

TWO *days after the Southern States had seceded, Lincoln sent this concise summation of the difference in Northern and Southern viewpoints to the man who was destined to assume the second highest office in the Confederacy.*

LETTER TO ALEXANDER H. STEPHENS

(For your own eye only.)

Springfield, Illinois, December 22, 1860

MY DEAR SIR:
    Your obliging answer to my short note is just received, and for which please accept my thanks. I fully appreciate the present peril the country is in, and the weight of responsibility on me. Do the people of the South really entertain fears that a Republican administration would, directly or indirectly, interfere with the slaves, or with them about the slaves? If they do, I wish to

assure you, as once a friend, and still, I hope, not an enemy, that there is no cause for such fears. The South would be in no more danger in this respect than it was in the days of Washington. I suppose, however, this does not meet the case. You think slavery is right and ought to be extended, while we think it is wrong and ought to be restricted. That, I suppose, is the rub. It certainly is the only substantial difference between us.

Yours very truly,

A. LINCOLN

Lincoln's Farewell Address

"THERE *was an unusual quiver on his lip, and a still more unusual tear on his furrowed cheek," said Ward Lamon, who witnessed the sad parting when Lincoln, pausing on the rear platform of his train, addressed these few, unprepared words to his friends in Springfield.*

ADDRESS AT SPRINGFIELD
FEB. 11, 1861

MY FRIENDS:

No one, not in my situation, can appreciate my feeling of sadness at this parting. To this place, and the kindness of these people, I owe everything. Here I have lived a quarter of a century, and have passed from a young to an old man. Here my children have been born, and one is buried. I now leave, not knowing when or whether ever I may return, with a task before me greater than that which rested upon Washington. Without the assistance of that Divine Being who ever attended him, I cannot succeed. With that assistance, I cannot fail. Trusting in Him who can go with me, and remain with you, and be everywhere for good, let us confidently hope that all will yet be well. To His care commending you, as I hope in your prayers you will commend me, I bid you an affectionate farewell.

~~~~~~

"... shall the liberties of this Country be preserved?"

~~~~~~

WHEN *the Presidential train stopped at Indianapolis on its way to Washington, Lincoln delivered this abbreviated address, reminding the people that the preservation of liberty was their business and not his.*

ADDRESS AT INDIANAPOLIS
FEB. 11, 1861

GOVERNOR MORTON and Fellow-citizens of the State of Indiana: Most heartily do I thank you for this magnificent reception; and while I cannot take to myself any share of the compliment thus paid, more than that which pertains to a mere instrument—an accidental instrument perhaps I should say—of a great cause, I yet must look upon it as a magnificent reception, and as such most heartily do I thank you for it. You have been pleased to address yourself to me chiefly in behalf of this glorious Union in which we live, in all of which you have my hearty sympathy, and, as far as may be within my power, will have, one and inseparably, my hearty coöperation. While I do not expect, upon this occasion, or until I get to Washington, to attempt any lengthy speech, I will only say that to the salvation of the Union there needs but one single thing, the hearts of a people like yours. When the people rise in mass in behalf of the Union and the liberties of this country, truly may it be said, "The gates of hell cannot prevail against them." In all trying positions in which I shall be placed, and doubtless I shall be placed in many such, my reliance will be upon you and the people of the United States; and I wish you to remember, now and forever, that it is your business, and not mine; that if the union of these States and the liberties of this people shall be lost, it is but little to any one man of fifty-two years of age, but a great deal to the thirty millions of people who inhabit these United States, and to their posterity in all coming time. It is your business to rise up and preserve the Union and liberty for yourselves, and not for me. I appeal to you again to constantly bear in mind that not with politicians, not with

Presidents, not with office-seekers, but with you, is the question: Shall the Union and shall the liberties of this country be preserved to the latest generations?

Speech at Independence Hall

DETECTIVE *Allan Pinkerton intercepted the Presidential party at Philadelphia to warn Lincoln of a plot for his assassination. Speaking that evening at Independence Hall, Lincoln had proclaimed he would rather be assassinated on the spot than sacrifice the principles of the Declaration of Independence.*

ADDRESS AT PHILADELPHIA
FEB. 22, 1861

MR. CUYLER:

I am filled with deep emotion at finding myself standing in this place, where were collected together the wisdom, the patriotism, the devotion to principle, from which sprang the institutions under which we live. You have kindly suggested to me that in my hands is the task of restoring peace to our distracted country. I can say in return, sir, that all the political sentiments

I entertain have been drawn, so far as I have been able to draw them, from the sentiments which originated in and were given to the world from this hall. I have never had a feeling, politically, that did not spring from the sentiments embodied in the Declaration of Independence. I have often pondered over the dangers which were incurred by the men who assembled here and framed and adopted that Declaration. I have pondered over the toils that were endured by the officers and soldiers of the army who achieved that independence. I have often inquired of myself what great principle or idea it was that kept this Confederacy so long together. It was not the mere matter of separation of the colonies from the motherland, but that sentiment in the Declaration of Independence which gave liberty not alone to the people of this country, but hope to all the world, for all future time. It was that which gave promise that in due time the weights would be lifted from the shoulders of all men, and that all should have an equal chance. This is the sentiment embodied in the Declaration of Independence. Now, my friends, can this country be saved on that basis? If it can, I will consider myself one of the happiest men in the world if I can help to save it. If it cannot be saved upon that principle, it will be truly awful. But if this country cannot be saved without giving up that principle, I was about to say I would rather be assassinated on this spot than surrender it. Now, in my view of the present aspect of affairs, there is no need of bloodshed and war. There is no necessity for it. I am not in favor of such a course; and I may say in advance that there will be no bloodshed unless it is forced upon the government. The government will not use force, unless force is used against it.

My friends, this is wholly an unprepared speech. I did not expect to be called on to say a word when I came here. I supposed I was merely to do something toward raising a flag. I may, therefore, have said something indiscreet. But I have said nothing but what I am willing to live by, and, if it be the pleasure of Almighty God, to die by.

"I feel constrained to beg. . . ."

WHEN *Lincoln refused to let Seward dictate the members of his Cabinet, the Secretary of State handed in his resignation. Saying, "I can't afford to let Seward take the first trick," the President immediately dispatched this note.*

LETTER TO WILLIAM H. SEWARD

Executive Mansion, March 4, 1861

MY DEAR SIR:

Your note of the 2d instant, asking to withdraw your acceptance of my invitation to take charge of the State Department, was duly received. It is the subject of the most painful solicitude with me, and I feel constrained to beg that you will countermand the withdrawal. The public interest, I think, demands that you should; and my personal feelings are deeply enlisted in the same direction. Please consider and answer by 9 A.M. to-morrow.

Your obedient servant,

A. LINCOLN

"Some Thoughts for the President's Consideration"

BELIEVING *the President incompetent to run the affairs of State in times of crisis, Secretary Seward attempted to take over the reins by submitting a detailed plan of action. Said the noted Civil War journalist, Henry Watterson, in commenting on Lincoln's reply, "Not a word was omitted that was necessary, and not a hint or allusion is contained that could be dispensed with. It was conclusive."*

LETTER TO WILLIAM H. SEWARD

Executive Mansion, April 1, 1861

MY DEAR SIR:

Since parting with you I have been considering your paper dated this day, and entitled "Some Thoughts for the President's Consideration." The first proposition in it is, *"First, We are at the end of a month's administration,* and yet without a policy either domestic or foreign."

At the beginning of that month, in the inaugural, I said: "The power confided in me will be used to hold, occupy, and possess the property and places belonging to the government, and to collect the duties and imposts." This had your distinct approval at the time; and, taken in connection with the order I immediately gave General Scott, directing him to employ every means in his power to strengthen and hold the forts, comprises the exact domestic policy you now urge, with the single exception that it does not propose to abandon Fort Sumter.

Again, I do not perceive how the reinforcement of Fort Sumter would be done on a slavery or a party issue, while that of Fort Pickens would be on a more national and patriotic one.

The news received yesterday in regard to St. Domingo certainly brings a new item within the range of our foreign policy; but up to that time we have been preparing circulars and instructions to ministers and the like, all in perfect harmony, without even a suggestion that we had no foreign policy.

Upon your closing propositions—that "whatever policy we adopt, there must be an energetic prosecution of it.

"For this purpose it must be somebody's business to pursue and direct it incessantly.

"Either the President must do it himself, and be all the while active in it, or

"Devolve it on some member of his cabinet. Once adopted, debates on it must end, and all agree and abide"—I remark that if this must be done, I must do it. When a general line of policy is adopted, I apprehend there is no danger of its being changed without good reason, or continuing to be a subject of unnecessary debate; still, upon points arising in its progress I wish, and suppose I am entitled to have, the advice of all the cabinet.

Your obedient servant,

A. LINCOLN

"... pecuniarily responsible. ..."

WISHING *neither to hurt the feelings of a man who requested a letter of recommendation nor to mislead his friend Swett, Lincoln carefully and shrewdly worded this note to serve both purposes.*

LETTER TO LEONARD SWETT

HON. L. SWETT

DEAR SIR:
This introduces Mr. William Yates, who visits Bloomington on some business matter. He is pecuniarily responsible for anything he will say; and, in fact, for anything he will say on any subject.

Yours very truly,

A. LINCOLN

~~~~~~

"*You will hold out if possible....*"

~~~~~~

THIS *letter was addressed to the besieged Union forces at Fort Sumter. Drafted by the President and signed by the Secretary of War, it bore an indorsement in Lincoln's handwriting reading, "This was sent by Captain Talbot on April 6, 1861, to be delivered to Major Anderson, if permitted. On reaching Charleston, he was refused permission to deliver it to Major Anderson."*

LETTER TO MAJOR ROBERT ANDERSON

War Department, Washington, April 4, 1861

SIR:
     Your letter of the 1st instant occasions some anxiety to the President.

On the information of Captain Fox, he had supposed you could hold out till the 15th instant without any great inconvenience, and had prepared an expedition to relieve you before that period.

Hoping still that you will be able to sustain yourself till the 11th or 12th instant, the expedition will go forward, and, finding your flag flying, will attempt to provision you, and in case the effort is resisted, will endeavor also to reinforce you.

You will therefore hold out, if possible, till the arrival of the expedition.

It is not, however, the intention of the President to subject your command to any danger or hardship beyond what, in your judgment, would be usual in military life; and he has entire confidence that you will act as becomes a patriot and a soldier under all circumstances.

Whenever, if at all, in your judgment, to save yourself and command, a capitulation becomes a necessity, you are authorized to make it.

Respectfully,

SIMON CAMERON

~~~~~~

"For a daring and dangerous enterprise. . . ."

~~~~~~

IT was such letters as this, written to Gustavus Fox after his failure to provision Fort Sumter, that won for Lincoln the loyal devotion and supreme efforts of his commanders.

LETTER TO GUSTAVUS V. FOX

Washington, May 1, 1861

MY DEAR SIR:

I sincerely regret that the failure of the late attempt to provision Fort Sumter should be the source of any annoyance to you.

The practicability of your plan was not, in fact, brought to a test. By reason of a gale, well known in advance to be possible and not improbable, the tugs, an essential part of the plan, never reached the ground; while, by an accident for which you were in no wise responsible, and possibly I to some extent was, you were deprived of a war vessel, with her men, which you deemed of great importance to the enterprise.

I most cheerfully and truly declare that the failure of the undertaking has not lowered you a particle, while the qualities you developed in the effort have greatly heightened you in my estimation.

For a daring and dangerous enterprise of a similar character you would to-day be the man of all my acquaintances whom I would select. You and I both anticipated that the cause of the country would be advanced by making the attempt to provision Fort Sumter, even if it should fail; and it is no small consolation now to feel that our anticipation is justified by the result.

Very truly your friend,

A. LINCOLN

"... beyond all earthly power."

LINCOLN *had a fatherly affection for Colonel Ellsworth, who, in the early days of the war, was fatally shot while lowering a Confederate flag from the roof of a house in Alexandria, Virginia. Lincoln's letter to the young officer's parents ranks with the famous Bixby letter as a masterpiece of compassion.*

LETTER TO COLONEL ELLSWORTH'S PARENTS

Washington, D. C., May 25, 1861

MY DEAR SIR AND MADAM:
In the untimely loss of your noble son, our affliction here is scarcely less than your own. So much of promised usefulness to one's country, and of bright hopes for one's self and friends, have rarely been so suddenly dashed as in his fall. In size, in years, and in youthful appearance a boy only, his power to command men

[110]

was surpassingly great. This power, combined with a fine intellect, an indomitable energy, and a taste altogether military, constituted in him, as seemed to me, the best natural talent in that department I ever knew.

And yet he was singularly modest and deferential in social intercourse. My acquaintance with him began less than two years ago; yet through the latter half of the intervening period it was as intimate as the disparity of our ages and my engrossing engagements would permit. To me he appeared to have no indulgences or pastimes; and I never heard him utter a profane or an intemperate word. What was conclusive of his good heart, he never forgot his parents. The honors he labored for so laudably, and for which in the sad end he so gallantly gave his life, he meant for them no less than for himself.

In the hope that it may be no intrusion upon the sacredness of your sorrow, I have ventured to address you this tribute to the memory of my young friend and your brave and early fallen child.

May God give you that consolation which is beyond all earthly power.

Sincerely your friend in a common affliction,

A. LINCOLN

―――――――――――――――――――――――――――

"Wanting to work is so rare. . . ."

―――――――――――――――――――――――――――

LINCOLN *grants the request of a mother seeking employ-*
ment for her two sons.

LETTER TO MAJOR RAMSEY

Executive Mansion, October 17, 1861

MY DEAR SIR:
The lady bearer of this says she has
two sons who want to work. Set them at it if possible. Wanting to work is so rare a want that it
should be encouraged.

Yours truly,

A. LINCOLN

"Hadn't we better spank this drummer boy ... ?"

Lincoln *recommends a more appropriate punishment to fit the crime of 14-year old Daniel Winger who had been sentenced to be shot.*

LETTER TO EDWIN M. STANTON

MY DEAR SIR:
Hadn't we better spank this drummer boy and send him back home to Leavenworth?

A. Lincoln

"He who does something at the head of one regiment. . . ."

WHEN *Major-General Hunter was assigned the command of the Department of Kansas he considered the appointment far beneath his capacity and wrote the President saying so. On Lincoln's answering letter the General made this notation: "The President's reply to my 'ugly letter.' This lay on his table a month after it was written, and when finally sent was by a special conveyance, with the direction that it was only to be given to me when I was in good humor."*

LETTER TO MAJOR-GENERAL HUNTER

Executive Mansion, Washington, December 31, 1861

DEAR SIR:

Yours of the 23d is received, and I am constrained to say it is difficult to answer so ugly a letter in good temper. I am, as you intimate, losing much of the great confidence I placed in you, not from any act or omission of yours touching the public service, up to the time you were sent to Leavenworth, but from the flood of grumbling despatches and letters I have seen from you since. I knew you were being ordered to Leavenworth at the time it was done; and I aver that with as tender a regard for your honor and your sensibilities as I had for my own, it never occurred to me that you were being "humiliated, insulted and disgraced!" nor have I, up to this day, heard an intimation that you have been wronged, coming from any one but yourself. No one has blamed you for the retrograde movement from Springfield, nor for the information you gave General Cameron; and this you could readily understand, if it were not for your unwarranted assumption that the ordering you to Leavenworth must necessarily have been done as a *punishment* for some *fault*. I thought then, and think yet, the position assigned to you is as responsible, and as honorable, as that assigned to Buell—I know that General McClellan expected more important results from it. My impression is that at the time you were assigned to the new Western Department, it had not been determined to replace General Sherman in Kentucky; but of this I am not certain, because the idea that a command in Kentucky was very desirable, and one in the farther West undesirable, had never occurred to me. You constantly speak of being placed in command of only 3,000. Now tell me, is this not mere impatience? Have you not known all the while that you are to command four or five times that many?

I have been, and am sincerely your friend; and if, as such, I dare to make a suggestion, I would say you are adopting the best possible way to ruin yourself. "Act well your part, there all the honor lies." He who does *something* at the head of one Regiment, will eclipse him who does *nothing* at the head of a hundred.

Your friend, as ever,

A. LINCOLN

Executive Mansion
Oct 17, 1861

Major Ramsey,
  My dear Sir
    The lady — bearer of
this — says she has two sons.
who want to work — Set them
at it, if possible — Wanting
to work is so rare a merit,
that it should be encouraged
     Yours truly
     A, Lincoln

An excellent example of Lincoln's faculty for in-
jecting wit and wisdom into routine correspondence. From the Oliver R. Barrett collection.

~~~~~~

"*I wish to be free to go at once.* . . ."

~~~~~~

LINCOLN *advises the Secretary of War that the precautions taken for the safety of the President are neither necessary nor convenient.*

LETTER TO EDWIN M. STANTON

Executive Mansion, January 22, 1862

MY DEAR SIR:

On reflection I think it will not do, as a rule, for the adjutant-general to attend me wherever I go: not that I have any objection to his presence, but that it would be an uncompensating encumbrance both to him and me. When it shall occur to me to go anywhere, I wish to be free to go at once, and not to have to notify the adjutant-general and wait till he can get ready.

It is better, too, for the public service that he shall give his time to the business of his office, and not to personal attendance on me.

While I thank you for the kindness of the suggestion, my view of the matter is as I have stated.

Yours truly,

A. LINCOLN

"... the Commander-in-Chief may order what he pleases."

WHEN *he found it necessary to over-rule General Mc-Clellan, Lincoln was direct and firm, but careful not to offend his sensitive commander.*

LETTER TO GEORGE B. McCLELLAN

Executive Mansion, March 21, 1862

MY DEAR SIR:

This morning I felt constrained to order Blenker's division to Fremont, and I write this to assure you that I did so with great pain, understanding that you would wish it otherwise. If you could know the full pressure of the case, I am confident you would justify it, even beyond a mere acknowledgment that the Commander-in-Chief may order what he pleases.

Yours, very truly,

ABRAHAM LINCOLN

"... a safe place for certain men to stand on the Constitution. ..."

LINCOLN *decries the acts of a judge who uses the protection of the Constitution to shield certain men who would seek to destroy it.*

LETTER TO JOHN W. CRISFIELD

Executive Mansion, Washington, June 26, 1862

MY DEAR SIR:

I have been considering the appeal made by yourself and Senator Pearce in behalf of Judge Carmichael. His charge to the Grand Jury was left with me by the senator, and on reading it I must confess I was not very favorably impressed toward the judge. The object of the charge, I understand, was to procure prosecution and punishment of some men for arresting or doing violence to some secessionists—that is, the judge was trying to help a little by giving the protection of law to those who were endeavoring to overthrow the supreme law—trying if he could find a safe place for certain men to stand on the Constitution, whilst they should stab it in another place.

But possibly I am mistaken.

The Secretary of War and I have agreed that if the judge will take the oath of allegiance usually taken in such cases, he may be discharged. Please ascertain and inform me whether he will do it.

Yours very truly,

A. LINCOLN

"My view of the present condition of the war. . . ."

~~~~~~

THIS *letter is one of three selected by John G. Nicolay,*
the President's secretary and biographer, as being representa-
tive of "Lincoln at his best."

LETTER TO WILLIAM H. SEWARD

Executive Mansion, June 28, 1862

M Y DEAR SIR:
My view of the present condition of
the war is about as follows:

The evacuation of Corinth and our delay by
the flood in the Chickahominy have enabled the
enemy to concentrate too much force in Richmond
for McClellan to successfully attack. In fact there
soon will be no substantial rebel force anywhere
else. But if we send all the force from here to Mc-
Clellan, the enemy will, before we can know of
it, send a force from Richmond and take Wash-

ington. Or if a large part of the western army be brought here to McClellan, they will let us have Richmond, and retake Tennessee, Kentucky, Missouri, etc. What should be done is to hold what we have in the West, open the Mississippi, and take Chattanooga and East Tennessee without more. A reasonable force should in every event be kept about Washington for its protection. Then let the country give us a hundred thousand new troops in the shortest possible time, which, added to McClellan directly or indirectly, will take Richmond without endangering any other place which we now hold, and will substantially end the war. I expect to maintain this contest until successful, or till I die, or am conquered, or my term expires, or Congress or the country forsake me; and I would publicly appeal to the country for this new force were it not that I fear a general panic and stampede would follow, so hard it is to have a thing understood as it really is. I think the new force should be all, or nearly all, infantry, principally because such can be raised most cheaply and quickly.

Yours very truly,

A. Lincoln

~~~~~~

"I am a patient man. . . ."

~~~~~~

LINCOLN'S *patience is sorely tried in answering Reverdy Johnson, Baltimore Unionist, who had joined the chorus of criticism of the Louisiana Military Authority.*

LETTER TO REVERDY JOHNSON

(*Private*)

Executive Mansion, Washington, July 26, 1862

MY DEAR SIR:
Yours of the 16th, by the hand of Governor Shepley, is received. It seems the Union feeling in Louisiana is being crushed out by the course of General Phelps. Please pardon me for believing that is a false pretense. The people of Louisiana—all intelligent people everywhere—know full well that I never had a wish to touch the foundations of their society, or any right of theirs. With perfect knowledge of this they forced

a necessity upon me to send armies among them, and it is their own fault, not mine, that they are annoyed by the presence of General Phelps. They also know the remedy—know how to be cured of General Phelps. Remove the necessity of his presence. And might it not be well for them to consider whether they have not already had time enough to do this? If they can conceive of anything worse than General Phelps within my power, would they not better be looking out for it? They very well know the way to avert all this is simply to take their place in the Union upon the old terms. If they will not do this, should they not receive harder blows rather than lighter ones? You are ready to say I apply to friends what is due only to enemies. I distrust the wisdom if not the sincerity of friends who would hold my hands while my enemies stab me. This appeal of professed friends has paralyzed me more in this struggle than any other one thing. You remember telling me, the day after the Baltimore mob in April, 1861, that it would crush all Union feeling in Maryland for me to attempt bringing troops over Maryland soil to Washington. I brought the troops notwithstanding, and yet there was Union feeling enough left to elect a legislature the next autumn, which in turn elected a very excellent Union United States senator! I am a patient man—always willing to forgive on the Christian terms of repentance, and also to give ample time for repentance. Still, I must save this government, if possible. What I cannot do, of course I will not do; but it may as well be understood, once for all, that I shall not surrender this game leaving any available card unplayed.

Yours truly,

A. LINCOLN

~~~~~~

"Broken eggs cannot be mended...."

~~~~~~

H IS *dander up, Lincoln replies vigorously to another critic of the government's Louisiana policy, through August Belmont, the New York financier.*

LETTER TO AUGUST BELMONT

July 31, 1862

D EAR SIR:

You send to Mr. W—— an extract from a letter written at New Orleans the 9th instant, which is shown to me. You do not give the writer's name; but plainly he is a man of ability, and probably of some note. He says: "The time has arrived when Mr. Lincoln must take a decisive course. Trying to please everybody, he will satisfy nobody. A vacillating policy in matters of importance is the very worst. Now is the time, if ever, for honest men who love their country to rally to its support. Why will not the North say officially that it wishes for the restoration of the Union as it was?"

And so, it seems, this is the point on which the writer thinks I have no policy. Why will he not read and understand what I have said?

The substance of the very declaration he desires is in the inaugural, in each of the two regular messages to Congress, and in many, if not all, the minor documents issued by the Executive since the inauguration.

Broken eggs cannot be mended; but Louisiana has nothing to do now but to take her place in the Union as it was, barring the already broken eggs. The sooner she does so, the smaller will be the amount of that which will be past mending. This government cannot much longer play a game in which it stakes all, and its enemies stake nothing. Those enemies must understand that they cannot experiment for ten years trying to destroy the government, and if they fail still come back into the Union unhurt. If they expect in any contingency to ever have the Union as it was, I join with the writer in saying, "Now is the time."

How much better it would have been for the writer to have gone at this, under the protection of the army at New Orleans, than to have sat down in a closet writing complaining letters northward!

Yours truly,

A. LINCOLN

"Can't you give him a chance?"

CARL SANDBURG, *in his "War Years," tells of the time Lincoln met a man in the street and said, "You look like an able-bodied man—why don't you join the army?" When the man answered that he'd be glad to die for his country if only given a chance, Lincoln wrote out and sealed this note, addressed to 714 Fifteenth Street, and instructed the man to take it there.*

NOTE TO COLONEL FIELDING

COL. FIELDING—

The bearer is anxious to go to the front and die for his country. Can't you give him a chance?

A. LINCOLN

"I would save the Union."

WHEN *the New York* Tribune *assailed the President editorially for not taking a more radical stand on the question of slavery, Lincoln sent to Horace Greeley this famous reply, which ranks near the top of his greatest State Papers.*

LETTER TO HORACE GREELEY

Executive Mansion, Washington, August, 22, 1862

DEAR SIR:

I have just read yours of the 19th, addressed to myself through the New York "Tribune." If there be in it any statements or assumptions of fact which I may know to be erroneous, I do not now and here, controvert them. If there be in it any inferences which I may believe to be falsely drawn, I do not, now and here, argue against them. If there be perceptible in it an impatient and dictatorial tone, I waive it in deference to an old friend whose heart I have always supposed to be right.

As to the policy I "seem to be pursuing," as you say, I have not meant to leave any one in doubt.

I would save the Union. I would save it the shortest way under the Constitution. The sooner the national authority can be restored, the nearer the Union will be "the Union as it was." If there be those who would not save the Union unless they could at the same time save slavery, I do not agree with them. If there be those who would not save the Union unless they could at the same time destroy slavery, I do not agree with them. My paramount object in this struggle is to save the Union, and is not either to save or to destroy slavery. If I could save the Union without freeing any slave, I would do it; and if I could save it by freeing all the slaves, I would do it; and if I could save it by freeing some and leaving others alone, I would also do that. What I do about slavery and the colored race, I do because I believe it helps to save the Union; and what I forbear, I forbear because I do not believe it would help to save the Union. I shall do less whenever I shall believe what I am doing hurts the cause, and I shall do more whenever I shall believe doing more will help the cause. I shall try to correct errors when shown to be errors, and I shall adopt new views so fast as they shall appear to be true views.

I have here stated my purpose according to my view of official duty; and I intend no modification of my oft-expressed personal wish that all men everywhere could be free.

Yours,

A. LINCOLN

"These are not the days of miracles. . . ."

ALTHOUGH *in this reply to a religious delegation Lincoln explained why he should not issue an Emancipation Proclamation, he had at that very moment a draft of the Proclamation in his desk and was only holding it for the right occasion. Three days later the Battle of Antietam provided the long-awaited opportunity, and on September 24 Lincoln released the Proclamation to the press.*

REPLY TO INTERDENOMINATIONAL RELIGIOUS COMMITTEE

September 13, 1862

THE subject presented in the memorial is one upon which I have thought much for weeks past, and I may even say for months. I am approached with the most opposite opinions and advice, and that by religious men who are equally certain that they represent the divine will. I am sure that either the one or the other class is mistaken in that belief, and perhaps in some respects both. I hope it will not be irreverent for me to say that if it is probable that God would reveal his will to others on a point so connected with my duty, it might be supposed he would reveal it directly to me; for, unless I am more deceived in myself than I often am, it is my earnest desire to know the will of Providence in this matter. And if I can learn what it is, I will do it.

These are not, however, the days of miracles, and I suppose it will be granted that I am not to expect a direct revelation. I must study the plain physical facts of the case, ascertain what is possible, and learn what appears to be wise and right.

The subject is difficult, and good men do not agree. For instance, the other day four gentlemen of standing and intelligence from New York called as a delegation on business connected with the war; but, before leaving, two of them earnestly beset me to proclaim general emancipation, upon which the other two at once attacked them. You know also that the last session of Congress had a decided majority of anti-slavery men, yet they could not unite on this policy. And the same is true of the religious people. Why, the rebel soldiers are praying with a great deal more earnestness, I fear, than our own troops, and expecting God to favor their side; for one of our soldiers who had been taken prisoner told Senator Wilson a few days since that he met with nothing so discouraging as the evident sincerity of those he was among in their prayers. But we will talk over the merits of the case.

What good would a proclamation of emancipation from me do, especially as we are now situated? I do not want to issue a document that the whole world will see must necessarily be inoperative, like the Pope's bull against the comet. Would my word free the slaves, when I cannot even enforce the Constitution in the rebel States? Is there a single court, or magistrate, or individual that would be influenced by it there? And what reason is there to think it would have any greater effect upon the slaves than the late law of Congress, which I approved, and which offers protection and freedom to the slaves of rebel masters who come within our lines? Yet I cannot learn that that law has caused a single slave to come over to us. And suppose they could be induced by a proclamation of freedom from me to throw themselves upon us, what should we do with them? How can we feed and care for such a multitude? General Butler wrote me a few days since that he was issuing more rations to the slaves who have rushed to him than to all the white troops under his command. They eat, and that is all; though it is true General Butler is feeding the whites also by the thousand, for it nearly amounts to a famine there. If, now, the pressure of the war should call off our forces from New Orleans to defend some other point, what is to prevent the masters from reducing the blacks to slavery again? For I am told that whenever the rebels take any black prisoners, free or slave, they immediately auction them off. They did so with those they took from a boat that was aground in the Tennessee River a few days ago. And then I am very ungenerously attacked for it! For instance, when, after the late battles at and near Bull Run, an expedition went out from Washington under a flag of truce to bury the dead and bring in the wounded, and the rebels seized the blacks who went along to help, and sent them into slavery, Horace Greeley said in his paper that the government would probably do nothing about it. What could I do?

Now, then, tell me, if you please, what possible result of good would follow the issuing of such a proclamation as you desire? Understand, I raise no objections against it on legal or constitutional grounds; for, as commander-in-chief of the army and navy, in time of war I suppose I have a right to take any measure which may best subdue the enemy; nor do I urge objections of a moral nature, in view of possible consequences of insurrection and massacre at the South.

I view this matter as a practical war measure, to be decided on according to the advantages or disadvantages it may offer to the suppression of the rebellion.

I admit that slavery is the root of the rebellion, or at least its *sine qua non*. The ambition of politicians may have instigated them to act, but they would have been impotent without slavery as their instrument. I will also concede that emancipation would help us in Europe, and convince them that we are incited by something more than ambition. I grant, further, that it would help somewhat at the North, though not so much, I fear, as you and those you represent imagine. Still some additional strength would be added in that way to the war, and then, unquestionably, it would weaken the rebels by drawing off their laborers, which is of great importance; but I am not so sure we could do much with the blacks. If we were to arm them, I fear that in a few weeks the arms would be in the hands of the rebels; and, indeed, thus far we have not had arms enough to equip our white troops. I will mention another thing, though it meet only your scorn and contempt. There are fifty thousand bayonets in the Union armies from the border slave States. It would be a serious matter if, in consequence of a proclamation such as you desire, they should go over to the rebels. I do not think they all would—not so many, indeed, as a year ago, or six months ago—not so many to-day as yesterday. Every day increases their Union feeling. They are also getting their pride enlisted, and want to beat the rebels.

Let me say one thing more: I think you should admit that we already have an important principle to rally and unite the people, in the fact that constitutional government is at stake. This is a fundamental idea going down about as deep as anything.

Do not misunderstand me because I have mentioned these objections. They indicate the difficulties that have thus far prevented my action in some such way as you desire. I have not decided against a proclamation of liberty to the slaves, but hold the matter under advisement; and I can assure you that the subject is on my mind, by day and night, more than any other. Whatever shall appear to be God's will, I will do. I trust that in the freedom with which I have canvassed your views I have not in any respect injured your feelings.

"... breath alone kills no rebels."

LINCOLN *writes Vice-President Hamlin that he is flattered by the comments on his Proclamation, but sadly disappointed in its results.*

LETTER TO HANNIBAL HAMLIN
(*Strictly Private*)

Executive Mansion, Washington, September 28, 1862

MY DEAR SIR:
Your kind letter of the 25th is just received. It is known to some that while I hope something from the proclamation, my expectations are not as sanguine as are those of some friends. The time for its effect southward has not come; but northward the effect should be instantaneous.

It is six days old, and while commendation in newspapers and by distinguished individuals is all that a vain man could wish, the stocks have declined, and troops come forward more slowly than ever. This, looked soberly in the face, is not very satisfactory. We have fewer troops in the field at the end of six days than we had at the beginning— the attrition among the old outnumbering the addition by the new. The North responds to the proclamation sufficiently in breath; but breath alone kills no rebels.

I wish I could write more cheerfully; nor do I thank you the less for the kindness of your letter.

Yours very truly,

A. Lincoln

~~~~~~

". . . hardly proper for me to make speeches."

~~~~~~

CALLED *upon for a speech at Frederick, Maryland, Lincoln reiterates his great aversion to speaking when he has nothing to say.*

SPEECH AT FREDERICK, MARYLAND

October 4, 1862

IN my present position it is hardly proper for me to make speeches. Every word is so closely noted that it will not do to make foolish ones, and I cannot be expected to be prepared to make sensible ones. If I were as I have been for most of my life, I might, perhaps, talk nonsense to you for half an hour, and it wouldn't hurt anybody. As it is, I can only return thanks for the compliment paid our cause. Please accept my sincere thanks for the compliment to our country.

". . . sore-tongued and fatigued horses."

LINCOLN, *despairing of ever getting McClellan to move against the enemy, chides his able but cautious commander in a terse telegraphic despatch.*

TELEGRAM TO
GENERAL GEORGE B. McCLELLAN

War Department, Washington City
October 24 [25?], 1862

MAJOR-GENERAL McCLELLAN:
     I have just read your despatch about sore-tongued and fatigued horses. Will you pardon me for asking what the horses of your army have done since the battle of Antietam that fatigues anything?

A. LINCOLN

"*I intend no injustice.*"

LINCOLN *attempts to smooth over the ruffled temper of McClellan but still pleads for action.*

TELEGRAM TO
GENERAL GEORGE B. McCLELLAN

Executive Mansion
Washington, October 27, 1862. 12:10 P.M.

MAJOR-GENERAL McCLELLAN:

Yours of yesterday received. Most certainly I intend no injustice to any, and if I have done any I deeply regret it. To be told, after more than five weeks' total inaction of the army, and during which period we sent to the army every fresh horse we possibly could, amounting in the whole to 7,918, that the cavalry horses were too much fatigued to move, presents a very cheerless, almost hopeless, prospect for the future, and it may have forced something of impatience in my dispatch. If not recruited and rested then, when could they ever be? I suppose the river is rising, and I am glad to believe you are crossing.

A. LINCOLN

". . . do not think this is an ill-natured letter. . . ."

D ESPERATELY *needing action, Lincoln pleads again and again with his Generals who seize every excuse for delay.*

LETTER TO GENERAL NATHANIEL P. BANKS

Executive Mansion
Washington, November 22, 1862

M Y DEAR GENERAL BANKS:

Early last week you left me in high hope with your assurance that you would be off with your expedition at the end of that week, or early in this. It is now the end of this, and I have just been overwhelmed and confounded with the sight of a requisition made by you which, I am assured, cannot be filled and got off within an hour short of two months. I inclose you a copy of the requisition, in some hope that it is not genuine—that you have never seen it. My dear general, this expanding and piling up of *impedimenta* has been, so far, almost our ruin, and will be our final ruin if it is not abandoned. If you had the articles of this requisition upon the wharf, with the necessary animals to make them of any use, and forage for the animals, you could not get vessels together in two weeks to carry the whole, to say nothing of your twenty thousand men; and having the vessels, you could not put the cargoes aboard in two weeks more. And, after all, where you are going you have no use for them. When you parted with me you had no such ideas in your mind. I know you had not, or you could not have expected to be off so soon as you said. You must get back to something like the plan you had then, or your expedition is a failure before you start. You must be off before Congress meets. You would be better off anywhere, and especially where you are going, for not having a thousand wagons doing nothing but hauling forage to feed the animals that draw them, and taking at least two thousand men to care for the wagons and animals, who otherwise might be two thousand good soldiers. Now, dear general, do not think this is an ill-natured letter; it is the very reverse. The simple publication of this requisition would ruin you.

Very truly your friend,

A. LINCOLN

"... I will make quick work with them."

WHEN *pay for troops in Massachusetts had been held up and Governor Andrew telegraphed that he could not get "quick work" from the paymasters responsible, Lincoln sent him this sizzling wire.*

TELEGRAM TO
GOVERNOR JOHN A. ANDREW

PLEASE say to these gentlemen that if they do not work quickly I will make quick work with them. In the name of all that is reasonable, how long does it take to pay a couple of regiments?

A. LINCOLN

~~~~~~

"Although you were not successful. . . ."

~~~~~~

L*INCOLN encourages the Army of the Potomac, after the Battle of Fredericksburg, where the Union forces suffered one of the most crushing defeats of the war.*

MESSAGE TO THE ARMY OF THE POTOMAC

Executive Mansion
Washington, December 22, 1862

TO THE ARMY OF THE POTOMAC:
I have just read your commanding general's report of the battle of Fredericksburg. Although you were not successful, the attempt was not an error, nor the failure other than accident. The courage with which you, in an open field, maintained the contest against an intrenched foe, and the consummate skill and success with which you crossed and recrossed the river in the face of the enemy, show that you possess all the qualities

[150]

of a great army, which will yet give victory to the cause of the country and of popular government.

Condoling with the mourners for the dead, and sympathizing with the severely wounded, I congratulate you that the number of both is comparatively so small.

I tender to you, officers and soldiers, the thanks of the nation.

A. LINCOLN

"In this sad world of ours. . . ."

LINCOLN *consoles the daughter of his friend, Colonel McCullough, who died heroically fighting with Grant's army in Mississippi.*

LETTER TO FANNY McCULLOUGH

Executive Mansion
Washington, December 23, 1862

DEAR FANNY:
It is with deep regret that I learn of the death of your kind and brave father, and especially that it is affecting your young heart beyond what is common in such cases. In this sad world of ours sorrow comes to all, and to the young it comes with bittered agony because it takes them unawares. The older have learned ever to expect it. I am anxious to afford some alleviation of your present distress. Perfect relief is not possible, ex-

cept with time. You cannot now realize that you will ever feel better. Is not this so? And yet it is a mistake. You are sure to be happy again. To know this, which is certainly true, will make you some less miserable now. I have had experience enough to know what I say, and you need only to believe it to feel better at once. The memory of your dear father, instead of an agony, will yet be a sad, sweet feeling in your heart, of a purer and holier sort than you have known before.

Please present my kind regards to your afflicted mother.

Your sincere friend,

A. LINCOLN

The Emancipation Proclamation

T︎HE *Emancipation Proclamation, premature though it was, Lincoln considered the crowning achievement of his labors. Secretary Seward records that on the first day of January, 1863, when the President was about to affix his signature to this great document, Lincoln said, "I have been shaking hands since nine o'clock this morning, and my right hand is nearly paralyzed. If my name ever goes into history, it will be for this act, and my whole soul is in it. If my hand trembles when I sign the Proclamation all who examine the document hereafter, will say, 'he hesitated.'" The President firmly inscribed his "Abraham Lincoln;" then looked up and said, "That will do."*

FINAL EMANCIPATION PROCLAMATION
JANUARY 1, 1863

BY THE PRESIDENT OF THE UNITED STATES OF AMERICA:

A PROCLAMATION

WHEREAS, on the twenty-second day of September, in the year of our Lord one thousand eight hundred and sixty-two, a proclamation was issued by the President of the United States, containing, among other things, the following, to wit:

"That on the first day of January, in the year of our Lord one thousand eight hundred and sixty-three, all persons held as slaves within any State, or designated part of a State, the people whereof shall then be in rebellion against the United States, shall be then, thenceforward, and forever free; and the Executive Government of the United States, including the military and naval authority thereof, will recognize and maintain the freedom of such persons, and will do no act or acts to repress such persons, or any of them, in any efforts they may make for their actual freedom.

"That the Executive will, on the first day of

January aforesaid, by proclamation, designate the States and parts of States, if any, in which the people thereof respectively shall then be in rebellion against the United States; and the fact that any State, or the people thereof, shall on that day be in good faith represented in the Congress of the United States by members chosen thereto at elections wherein a majority of the qualified voters of such State shall have participated, shall in the absence of strong countervailing testimony be deemed conclusive evidence that such State and the people thereof are not then in rebellion against the United States."

Now, therefore, I, Abraham Lincoln, President of the United States, by virtue of the power in me vested as commander-in-chief of the army and navy of the United States, in time of actual armed rebellion against the authority and government of the United States, and as a fit and necessary war measure for suppressing said rebellion, do, on this first day of January, in the year of our Lord one thousand eight hundred and sixty-three, and in accordance with my purpose so to do, publicly proclaimed for the full period of 100 days from the day first above mentioned, order and designate as the States and parts of States wherein the people thereof, respectively, are this day in rebellion against the United States, the following, to wit: Arkansas, Texas, Louisiana (except the parishes of St. Bernard, Plaquemines, Jefferson, St. John, St. Charles, St. James, Ascension, Assumption, Terre Bonne, Lafourche, St. Mary, St. Martin, and Orleans, including the city of New Orleans), Mississippi, Alabama, Florida, Georgia, South Carolina, North Carolina, and Virginia (except the forty-eight counties designated as West Virginia, and also the counties of Berkeley, Accomac, Northampton, Elizabeth City, York, Princess Anne, and Norfolk, including the cities of Norfolk and Portsmouth), and which excepted parts are for the present left precisely as if this proclamation were not issued.

And by virtue of the power and for the purpose aforesaid, I do order and declare that all persons held as slaves within said designated States and parts of States are, and henceforward shall be, free; and that the Executive Government of the United States, including the military and naval authorities thereof, will recognize and maintain the freedom of said persons.

And I hereby enjoin upon the people so declared to be free to abstain from all violence, unless in necessary self-defense; and I recommend to them that, in all cases where allowed, they labor faithfully for reasonable wages.

And I further declare and make known that such persons of suitable condition will be received into the armed service of the United States to garrison forts, positions, stations, and other places, and to man vessels of all sorts in said service.

And upon this act, sincerely believed to be an act of justice, warranted by the Constitution upon military necessity, I invoke the considerate judgment of mankind and the gracious favor of Almighty God.

In witness whereof, I have hereunto set my hand and caused the seal of the United States to be affixed.

> Done at the city of Washington, this first day of January, in the year of our Lord one thousand eight hundred and sixty-three, and of the independence of the United States of America the eighty-seventh.

> ABRAHAM LINCOLN

By the President:

WILLIAM H. SEWARD, Secretary of State

∿∿

"Let the churches take care of themselves."

∿∿

"*WHEN an individual in a church or out of it becomes dangerous to the public interest, he must be checked; but let the churches, as such, take care of themselves,*" counsels the President in a letter to his Commander of the Department of Missouri.

LETTER TO GENERAL SAMUEL R. CURTIS

Executive Mansion
Washington, January 2, 1863

MY DEAR SIR:
Yours of December 29 by the hand of Mr. Strong is just received. The day I telegraphed you suspending the order in relation to Dr. McPheeters, he, with Mr. Bates, the Attorney-General, appeared before me and left with me a copy of the order mentioned. The doctor also showed me the copy of an oath which he said he had taken,

which is, indeed, very strong and specific. He also verbally assured me that he had constantly prayed in church for the President and government, as he had always done before the present war. In looking over the recitals in your order, I do not see that this matter of prayer, as he states it, is negatived, nor that any violation of his oath is charged, nor, in fact, that anything specific is alleged against him. The charges are all general: that he has a rebel wife and rebel relations, that he sympathizes with rebels, and that he exercises rebel influence. Now, after talking with him, I tell you frankly I believe he does sympathize with the rebels, but the question remains whether such a man, of unquestioned good moral character, who has taken such an oath as he has, and cannot even be charged with violating it, and who can be charged with no other specific act or omission, can, with safety to the government, be exiled upon the suspicion of his secret sympathies. But I agree that this must be left to you, who are on the spot; and if, after all, you think the public good requires his removal, my suspension of the order is withdrawn, only with this qualification, that the time during the suspension is not to be counted against him. I have promised him this. But I must add that the United

States Government must not, as by this order, undertake to run the churches. When an individual in a church or out of it becomes dangerous to the public interest, he must be checked; but let the churches, as such, take care of themselves. It will not do for the United States to appoint trustees, supervisors, or other agents for the churches.

Yours very truly,

A. LINCOLN

~~~~~~

"I will risk the dictatorship. . . ."

~~~~~~

LINCOLN *was having nothing but trouble with the Army of the Potomac. McClellan had been too wary; Burnside had been too rash. And now the President was to have thrust upon him, by the pressure of a disapproving Senate, a general of questionable merit. In one of his most remarkable letters, Lincoln warns his new general, without resentment but with amazing directness, of the faults he must surmount if he is to succeed.*

LETTER TO "FIGHTING JOE" HOOKER

Executive Mansion
Washington, D. C., January 26, 1863

GENERAL:

I have placed you at the head of the Army of the Potomac. Of course I have done this upon what appear to me to be sufficient reasons. And yet I think it best for you to know that there are some things in regard to which, I am not quite satisfied with you. I believe you to be a brave and skilful soldier, which, of course, I like. I also believe you do not mix politics with your profession, in which you are right. You have confidence in yourself, which is a valuable, if not an indispensable quality. You are ambitious, which, within reasonable bounds, does good rather than harm. But I think that during Gen. Burnside's command of the Army, you have taken counsel of your ambition, and thwarted him as much as you could, in which you did a great wrong to the country, and to a most meritorious and honorable brother officer. I have heard, in such a way as to believe it, of your recently saying that both the army and the government needed a dictator. Of course it was not for this, but in spite of it, that I have given you the command. Only those generals who gain successes can set up dictators. What I now ask of you is military success, and I will risk the dictatorship. The government will support you to the utmost of its ability, which is neither more nor less than it has done and will do for all commanders. I much fear that the spirit which you have aided to infuse into the army, of criticising their commander and withholding confidence from him, will now turn upon you. I shall assist you as far as I can to put it down. Neither you nor Napoleon, if he were alive again, could get any good out of an army while such a spirit prevails in it; and now beware of rashness. Beware of rashness, but with energy and sleepless vigilance go forward and give us victories.

Yours very truly,

A. LINCOLN

~~~~~~

"You and I are substantially strangers. . . ."

~~~~~~

L INCOLN *makes a friendly overture to one of the bitterest enemies of his administration, Governor Seymour of New York.*

LETTER TO GOVERNOR HORATIO SEYMOUR

March, 1863

M Y DEAR SIR:

You and I are substantially strangers, and I write this chiefly that we may become better acquainted. I, for the time being, am at the head of a nation which is in great peril, and you are at the head of the greatest State of that nation. As to maintaining the nation's life and integrity, I assume and believe there cannot be a difference of purpose between you and me. If we should differ as to the means, it is important that such difference should be as small as possible; that it should not be enhanced by unjust suspicions on one side or the other. In the performance of my duty the cooperation of your State, as that of others, is needed—in fact, is indispensable. This alone is a sufficient reason why I should wish to be at a good understanding with you. Please write me at least as long a letter as this, of course saying in it just what you think fit.

A. LINCOLN

". . . like an ox jumped half over the fence. . . ."

KEEPING *an ever closer eye on the operations of his army, Lincoln warns General Hooker to be alert and not to fall into Lee's trap.*

TELEGRAM TO "FIGHTING JOE" HOOKER

Washington, June 5, 1863. 4 P.M.

MAJOR-GENERAL HOOKER:
Yours of to-day was received an hour ago. So much of professional military skill is requisite to answer it, that I have turned the task over to General Halleck. He promises to perform it with his utmost care. I have but one idea which I think worth suggesting to you, and that is, in case you find Lee coming to the north of the Rappahannock, I would by no means cross to the south of it. If he should leave a rear force at Fredericksburg, tempting you to fall upon it, it would fight

in intrenchments and have you at disadvantage, and so, man for man, worst you at that point, while his main force would in some way be getting an advantage of you northward. In one word, I would not take any risk of being entangled upon the river, like an ox jumped half over a fence and liable to be torn by dogs front and rear without a fair chance to gore one way or kick the other. If Lee would come to my side of the river, I would keep on the same side, and fight him or act on the defense, according as might be my estimate of his strength relatively to my own. But these are mere suggestions which I desire to be controlled by the judgment of yourself and General Halleck.

A. LINCOLN

"If you are besieged...."

AN *urgent S.O.S. from General Tyler draws a pertinent, if not impertinent, response from his much harried Commander-in-Chief.*

TELEGRAM TO GENERAL DANIEL TYLER

War Department, June 14, 1863

GENERAL TYLER, MARTINSBURG:
If you are besieged how do you despatch me? Why did you not leave before being besieged?

A. LINCOLN

Lincoln's Shortest Speech

THIS *one-sentence speech, delivered at the flag-raising before the Treasury Building, is very likely the briefest address ever given upon a public occasion.*

SPEECH BEFORE THE TREASURY BUILDING

THE part assigned to me is to raise the flag, which, if there be no fault in the machinery, I will do, and when up, it will be for the people to keep it up.

*"Beware of being assailed by one
and praised by the other."*

LINCOLN *tells his new Commander in Missouri how best
to preserve peace among the quarrelsome factions in his territory.*

LETTER TO GENERAL JOHN M. SCHOFIELD

Executive Mansion, May 27, 1863

MY DEAR SIR:
Having relieved General Curtis and
assigned you to the command of the Department
of the Missouri, I think it may be of some advantage for me to state to you why I did it. I did
not relieve General Curtis because of any full conviction that he had done wrong by commission
or omission. I did it because of a conviction in
my mind that the Union men of Missouri, con-
stituting, when united, a vast majority of the whole

people, have entered into a pestilent factional quarrel among themselves—General Curtis, perhaps not of choice, being the head of one faction and Governor Gamble that of the other. After months of labor to reconcile the difficulty, it seemed to grow worse and worse, until I felt it my duty to break it up somehow; and as I could not remove Governor Gamble, I had to remove General Curtis. Now that you are in the position, I wish you to undo nothing merely because General Curtis or Governor Gamble did it, but to exercise your own judgment, and do right for the public interest. Let your military measures be strong enough to repel the invader and keep the peace, and not so strong as to unnecessarily harass and persecute the people. It is a difficult role, and so much greater will be the honor if you perform it well. If both factions, or neither, shall abuse you, you will probably be about right. Beware of being assailed by one and praised by the other.

Yours truly,

A. LINCOLN

~~~~~~

"...this is a glorious theme...."

~~~~~~

IN *an impromptu speech Lincoln points to the many unique coincidences which occurred on the 4th of July, including the deaths of Presidents Jefferson, Adams, Monroe, and the victories just gained at Gettysburg and Vicksburg.*

RESPONSE TO A SERENADE

July 7, 1863

FELLOW-CITIZENS:

I am very glad indeed to see you tonight, and yet I will not say I thank you for this call; but I do most sincerely thank Almighty God for the occasion on which you have called. How long ago is it?—eighty-odd years since, on the Fourth of July, for the first time in the history of the world, a nation, by its representatives, assembled and declared, as a self-evident truth, "that all men are created equal." That was the birthday of the United States of America. Since then the Fourth of July has had several very peculiar recognitions. The two men most distinguished in the framing and support of the Declaration were Thomas Jefferson and John Adams—the one having penned it, and the other sustained it the most forcibly in debate—the only two of the fifty-five who signed it that were elected Presidents of the United States. Precisely fifty years after they put their hands to the paper, it pleased Almighty God to take both from this stage of action. This was indeed an extraordinary and remarkable event in our history. Another President, five years after, was called from this stage of existence on the same day and month of the year; and now on this last Fourth of July just passed, when we have a gigantic rebellion, at the bottom of which is an effort to overthrow the principle that all men are created equal, we have the surrender of a most powerful position and army on that very day. And not only so, but in a succession of battles in Pennsylvania, near to us, through three days, so rapidly fought that they might be called one great battle, on the first, second, and third of the month of July; and on the fourth the cohorts of those who opposed the Declaration that all men are created equal "turned tail" and run. Gentlemen, this is a glorious theme, and the occasion for a speech, but I am not prepared to make one worthy of the occasion. I would like to speak in terms of praise due to the many brave officers and soldiers who have fought in the cause of the Union and liberties of their country from the beginning of the war. These are trying occasions, not only in success, but for the want of success. I dislike to mention the name of one single officer, lest I might do wrong to those I might forget. Recent events bring up glorious names, and particularly prominent ones; but these I will not mention. Having said this much, I will now take the music.

"... you were right and I was wrong."

LINCOLN *expresses his appreciation for the all-important victory at Vicksburg and, with characteristic frankness, admits that his own theories had been proved wrong.*

LETTER TO ULYSSES S. GRANT

Executive Mansion, July 13, 1863

MY DEAR GENERAL:

I do not remember that you and I ever met personally. I write this now as a grateful acknowledgment for the almost inestimable service you have done the country. I wish to say a word further. When you first reached the vicinity of Vicksburg, I thought you should do what you finally did—march the troops across the neck, run the batteries with the transports, and thus go below; and I never had any faith, except a general hope that you knew better than I, that the Yazoo

Pass expedition and the like could succeed. When you got below and took Port Gibson, Grand Gulf, and vicinity, I thought you should go down the river and join General Banks, and when you turned northward, east of the Big Black, I feared it was a mistake. I now wish to make the personal acknowledgment that you were right and I was wrong.

Yours very truly,

A. LINCOLN

The Letter Lincoln Wrote But Did Not Send

MOST *military authorities agreed that had General Meade pursued his advantage after his victory at Gettysburg, the war might have been ended then and there. Overcome with grief, Lincoln wrote this reproachful letter—mild enough, in view of the magnitude of the error—but never sent it, knowing the loss to be irreparable.*

LETTER TO GENERAL GEORGE G. MEADE

Executive Mansion
Washington, D. C., July 14, 1863

MAJOR-GENERAL MEADE:
I have just seen your despatch to General Halleck, asking to be relieved of your command because of a supposed censure of mine. I am very, very grateful to you for the magnificent success you gave the cause of the country at Gettysburg; and I am sorry now to be the author of

the slightest pain to you. But I was in such deep distress myself that I could not restrain some expression of it. I have been oppressed nearly ever since the battles of Gettysburg by what appeared to be evidences that yourself and General Couch and General Smith were not seeking a collision with the enemy, but were trying to get him across the river without another battle. What these evidences were, if you please, I hope to tell you at some time when we shall both feel better. The case, summarily stated, is this: You fought and beat the enemy at Gettysburg and, of course, to say the least, his loss was as great as yours. He retreated, and you did not, as it seemed to me, pressingly pursue him; but a flood in the river detained him till, by slow degrees, you were again upon him. You had at least twenty thousand veteran troops directly with you, and as many more raw ones within supporting distance, all in addition to those who fought with you at Gettysburg, while it was not possible that he had received a single recruit, and yet you stood and let the flood run down, bridges be built, and the enemy move away at his leisure without attacking him. And Couch and Smith! The latter left Carlisle in time, upon all ordinary calculation, to have aided you in the last battle at Gettysburg, but he did not arrive. At the end of more than ten days, I believe twelve, under constant urging, he reached Hagerstown from Carlisle, which is not an inch over fifty-five miles, if so much, and Couch's movement was very little different.

Again, my dear general, I do not believe you appreciate the magnitude of the misfortune involved in Lee's escape. He was within your easy grasp, and to have closed upon him would, in connection with our other late successes, have ended the war. As it is, the war will be prolonged indefinitely. If you could not safely attack Lee last Monday, how can you possibly do so south of the river, when you can take with you very few more than two thirds of the force you then had in hand?

It would be unreasonable to expect, and I do not expect [that], you can now effect much. Your golden opportunity is gone, and I am distressed immeasurably because of it.

I beg you will not consider this a prosecution or persecution of yourself. As you had learned that I was dissatisfied, I have thought it best to kindly tell you why.

~~~~~~

"... *without criticism for what was not done.*"

~~~~~~

O*NE week after he has magnanimously withheld his letter of censure to General Meade, Lincoln informs General Howard that he is "profoundly grateful for what was done, without criticism for what was not done."*

LETTER TO GENERAL OLIVER O. HOWARD

Executive Mansion, July 21, 1863

M**Y DEAR GENERAL HOWARD:**
Your letter of the 18th is received. I was deeply mortified by the escape of Lee across the Potomac, because the substantial destruction of his army would have ended the war, and because I believed such destruction was perfectly easy—believed that General Meade and his noble army had expended all the skill, and toil, and blood, up to the ripe harvest, and then let the crop go to waste.

[181]

Perhaps my mortification was heightened because I had always believed—making my belief a hobby, possibly—that the main rebel army going north of the Potomac could never return, if well attended to; and because I was so greatly flattered in this belief by the operations at Gettysburg. A few days having passed, I am now profoundly grateful for what was done, without criticism for what was not done.

General Meade has my confidence as a brave and skilful officer and a true man.

Yours very truly,

A. LINCOLN

~~~~~~

"... they have the better right. ..."

~~~~~~

LINCOLN *seized every possible opportunity to express his gratitude to those "who bear the chief burthen of saving our country." This is the third of three letters selected by John G. Nicolay as representative of Lincoln at his best.*

LETTER TO POSTMASTER-GENERAL
MONTGOMERY BLAIR

Executive Mansion, July 24, 1863

SIR:

Yesterday little endorsements of mine went to you in two cases of postmasterships sought for widows whose husbands have fallen in the battles of this war. These cases occurring on the same day brought me to reflect more attentively than I had before done, as to what is fairly due from us here in the dispensing of patronage toward the men who, by fighting our battles, bear the chief

[183]

burthen of saving our country. My conclusion is that, other claims and qualifications being equal, they have the better right; and this is especially applicable to the disabled soldier and the deceased soldier's family.

Your obedient servant,

A. LINCOLN

*" . . . no successful appeal from the ballot
to the bullet. . . ."*

As *a rule, a message of more than six pages would not be
considered a model of brevity, but into this letter, written to
be read at a Republican meeting in Springfield, Lincoln com-
presses a lifetime of philosophy.*

LETTER TO JAMES C. CONKLING

Executive Mansion, August 26, 1863

MY DEAR SIR:
    Your letter inviting me to attend a
mass-meeting of unconditional Union men, to be
held at the capital of Illinois on the 3d day of
September has been received. It would be very
agreeable to me to thus meet my old friends at
my own home, but I cannot just now be absent
from here so long as a visit there would require.
    The meeting is to be of all those who maintain

unconditional devotion to the Union; and I am sure my old political friends will thank me for tendering, as I do, the nation's gratitude to those and other noble men whom no partisan malice or partisan hope can make false to the nation's life.

There are those who are dissatisfied with me. To such I would say: You desire peace, and you blame me that we do not have it. But how can we attain it? There are but three conceivable ways: First, to suppress the rebellion by force of arms. This I am trying to do. Are you for it? If you are, so far we are agreed. If you are not for it, a second way is to give up the Union. I am against this. Are you for it? If you are, you should say so plainly. If you are not for force, nor yet for dissolution, there only remains some imaginable compromise. I do not believe any compromise embracing the maintenance of the Union is now possible. All I learn leads to a directly opposite belief. The strength of the rebellion is its military, its army. That army dominates all the country and all the people within its range. Any offer of terms made by any man or men within that range, in opposition to that army, is simply nothing for the present, because such man or men have no power whatever to enforce their side of a compromise, if one were made with them.

To illustrate: Suppose refugees from the South and peace men of the North get together in convention, and frame and proclaim a compromise embracing a restoration of the Union. In what way can that compromise be used to keep Lee's army out of Pennsylvania? Meade's army can keep Lee's army out of Pennsylvania, and, I think, can ultimately drive it out of existence. But no paper compromise to which the controllers of Lee's army are not agreed can at all affect that army. In an effort at such compromise we should waste time which the enemy would improve to our disadvantage; and that would be all. A compromise, to be effective, must be made either with those who control the rebel army, or with the people first liberated from the domination of that army by the success of our own army. Now, allow me to assure you that no word or intimation from that rebel army, or from any of the men controlling it, in relation to any peace compromise, has ever come to my knowledge or belief. All charges and insinuations to the contrary are deceptive and groundless. And I promise you that if any such proposition shall hereafter come, it shall not be rejected and kept a secret from you. I freely acknowledge myself the servant of the people, according to the bond of service—the United States Constitution—and that, as such, I am responsible to them.

But to be plain. You are dissatisfied with me about the negro. Quite likely there is a difference of opinion between you and myself upon that subject. I certainly wish that all men could be free, while I suppose you do not. Yet, I have neither adopted nor proposed any measure which is not consistent with even your view, provided you are for the Union. I suggested compensated emancipation, to which you replied you wished not to be taxed to buy negroes. But I had not asked you to be taxed to buy negroes, except in such way as to save you from greater taxation to save the Union exclusively by other means.

You dislike the emancipation proclamation, and perhaps would have it retracted. You say it is unconstitutional. I think differently. I think the Constitution invests its commander-in-chief with the law of war in time of war. The most that can be said—if so much—is that slaves are property. Is there—has there ever been—any question that by the law of war, property, both of enemies and friends, may be taken when needed? And is it not needed whenever taking it helps us, or hurts the enemy? Armies, the world over, destroy enemies' property when they cannot use it; and even destroy their own to keep it from the enemy. Civilized belligerents do all in their power to help themselves or hurt the enemy, except a few things regarded as barbarous or cruel. Among the exceptions are the massacre of vanquished foes and non-combatants, male and female.

But the proclamation, as law, either is valid or is not valid. If it is not valid, it needs no retraction. If it is valid, it cannot be retracted any more than the dead can be brought to life. Some of you profess to think its retraction would operate favorably for the Union. Why better after the retraction than before the issue? There was more than a year and a half of trial to suppress the rebellion before the proclamation issued; the last one hundred days of which passed under an explicit notice that it was coming, unless averted by those in revolt returning to their allegiance. The war has certainly progressed as favorably for us since the issue of the proclamation as before.

You say you will not fight to free negroes. Some of them seem willing to fight for you; but no matter. Fight you, then, exclusively, to save the Union. I issued the proclamation on purpose to aid you in saving the Union. Whenever you shall have conquered all resistance to the Union, if I shall urge you to continue fighting, it will be an apt time then for you to declare you will not fight to free negroes.

I thought that in your struggle for the Union, to whatever extent the negroes should cease helping the enemy, to that extent it weakened the enemy in his resistance to you. Do you think differently? I thought that whatever negroes can be got to do as soldiers, leaves just so much less for white soldiers to do in saving the Union. Does it appear otherwise to you? But negroes, like other people, act upon motives. Why should they do anything for us if we will do nothing for them? If they stake their lives for us they must be prompted by the strongest motive, even the promise of freedom. And the promise, being made, must be kept.

The signs look better. The Father of Waters again goes unvexed to the sea. Thanks to the great Northwest for it. Nor yet wholly to them. Three hundred miles up they met New England, Empire, Keystone, and Jersey, hewing their way right and left. The sunny South, too, in more colors than one, also lent a hand. On the spot, their part of the history was jotted down in black and white.

The job was a great national one, and let none be banned who bore an honorable part in it. And while those who have cleared the great river may well be proud, even that is not all. It is hard to say that anything has been more bravely and well done than at Antietam, Murfreesboro', Gettysburg, and on many fields of lesser note. Nor must Uncle Sam's web-feet be forgotten. At all the watery margins they have been present. Not only on the deep sea, the broad bay, and the rapid river, but also up the narrow, muddy bayou, and wherever the ground was a little damp, they have been and made their tracks. Thanks to all: for the great republic—for the principle it lives by and keeps alive—for man's vast future—thanks to all.

Peace does not appear so distant as it did. I hope it will come soon, and come to stay: and so come as to be worth the keeping in all future time. It will then have been proved that among free men there can be no successful appeal from the ballot to the bullet, and that they who take such appeal are sure to lose their case and pay the cost. And then there will be some black men who can remember that with silent tongue, and clenched teeth, and steady eye, and well-poised bayonet,

they have helped mankind on to this great con-
summation, while I fear there will be some white
ones unable to forget that with malignant heart
and deceitful speech they strove to hinder it.

Still, let us not be over-sanguine of a speedy
final triumph. Let us be quite sober. Let us dili-
gently apply the means, never doubting that a
just God, in his own good time, will give us the
rightful result.

Yours very truly,

A. LINCOLN

~~~~~~

"... the plain truth. ..."

~~~~~~

GENERAL ROSECRANS, *Commander of the Army of Cumberland, was another "problem child" of Lincoln's. When the President's repeated prodding finally penetrated "Old Rosy's" skin, Lincoln was quick to apply the palliative.*

LETTER TO GENERAL
WILLIAM S. ROSECRANS

Executive Mansion, August 31, 1863

MY DEAR GENERAL ROSECRANS:
Yours of the 22d was received yesterday. When I wrote you before, I did [not] intend, nor do I now, to engage in an argument with you on military questions. You had informed me you were impressed through General Halleck that I was dissatisfied with you; and I could not bluntly deny that I was without unjustly implicating him. I therefore concluded to tell you the plain truth,

being satisfied the matter would thus appear much smaller than it would if seen by mere glimpses. I repeat that my appreciation of you has not abated. I can never forget whilst I remember anything that about the end of last year and beginning of this, you gave us a hard-earned victory, which, had there been a defeat instead, the nation could scarcely have lived over. Neither can I forget the check you so opportunely gave to a dangerous sentiment which was spreading in the North.

Yours as ever,

A. Lincoln

―――――――――――――――――――――――――――――――――

"This nation already has a quarter-master-general."

―――――――――――――――――――――――――――――――――

Lincoln's *unfailing sense of humor would sometimes get him into trouble, as in this amusing incident told by the two following dispatches.*

TELEGRAMS TO J. K. DUBOIS AND O. M. HATCH

Washington, September 13, 1863

HON. J. K. DUBOIS, HON. O. M. HATCH:
What nation do you desire General Allen to be made quarter-master-general of? This nation already has a quarter-master-general.

A. LINCOLN

Executive Mansion, September 22, 1863

HON. O. M. HATCH, HON. J. K. DUBOIS,
SPRINGFIELD, ILL.:

Your letter is just received. The particular form of my despatch was jocular, which I supposed you gentlemen knew me well enough to understand. General Allen is considered here as a very faithful and capable officer, and one who would be at least thought of for quartermaster-general if that office were vacant.

A. LINCOLN

~~~~~~

"*. . . by commission or omission. . . .*"

~~~~~~

THURLOW WEED'S *sudden coolness toward the President leads Lincoln to believe that he has in some way offended the prominent politico.*

LETTER TO THURLOW WEED

Executive Mansion, October 14, 1863

MY DEAR SIR:
I have been brought to fear recently that somehow, by commission or omission, I have caused you some degree of pain. I have never entertained an unkind feeling or a disparaging thought toward you; and if I have said or done anything which has been construed into such unkindness or disparagement, it has been misconstrued. I am sure if we could meet we would not part with any unpleasant impression on either side.
Yours as ever,
A. LINCOLN

"... if Frank Blair were my brother...."

To *Postmaster-General Montgomery Blair Lincoln writes a Chesterfieldian letter full of friendly advice for the welfare of Blair's brother.*

LETTER TO MONTGOMERY BLAIR

Executive Mansion
Washington, D. C., November 2, 1863

MY DEAR SIR:

Some days ago I understood you to say that your brother, General Frank Blair, desires to be guided by my wishes as to whether he will occupy his seat in Congress or remain in the field. My wish, then, is compounded of what I believe will be best for the country and best for him, and it is that he will come here, put his military commission in my hands, take his seat, go into caucus with our friends, abide the nominations, help elect the nominees, and thus aid to organize a House of Representatives which will really support the government in the war. If the result shall be the election of himself as Speaker, let him serve in that position; if not, let him retake his commission and return to the army. For the country this will heal a dangerous schism; for him it will relieve from a dangerous position. By a misunderstanding, as I think, he is in danger of being permanently separated from those with whom only he can ever have a real sympathy—the sincere opponents of slavery. It will be a mistake if he shall allow the provocations offered him by insincere time-servers to drive him out of the house of his own building. He is young yet. He has abundant talent—quite enough to occupy all his time without devoting any to temper. He is rising in military skill and usefulness. His recent appointment to the command of a corps by one so competent to judge as General Sherman proves this. In that line he can serve both the country and himself more profitably than he could as a member of Congress on the floor. The foregoing is what I would say if Frank Blair were my brother instead of yours.

Yours truly,

A. LINCOLN

"... here's your autograph."

ALTHOUGH *very likely apocryphal, and not consistent with Lincoln's usual courteous treatment of all requests for favors—no matter how small—this terse note is included because it has been so often quoted.*

LETTER QUOTED BY THE *WASHINGTON STAR*

DEAR MADAM:
When you ask from a stranger that which is of interest only to yourself, always enclose a stamp. There's your sentiment, and here's your autograph.

A. LINCOLN

"...not quite free from ridicule."

LINCOLN *assures the Shakespearean actor, James H. Hackett, that he need not be uneasy for having allowed one of the President's letters to get into the hands of the press.*

LETTER TO JAMES H. HACKETT
(Private)

Washington, D. C., November 2, 1863

MY DEAR SIR:

Yours of October 22 is received, as also was in due course that of October 3. I look forward with pleasure to the fulfilment of the promise made in the former.

Give yourself no uneasiness on the subject mentioned in that of the 22d.

My note to you I certainly did not expect to see in print; yet I have not been much shocked by the newspaper comments upon it. Those comments constitute a fair specimen of what has occurred to me through life. I have endured a great deal of ridicule without much malice; and have received a great deal of kindness, not quite free from ridicule. I am used to it.

Yours truly,

A. LINCOLN

~~~~~~

"...the exact shade of Julius Caesar's hair."

~~~~~~

MANY *different interpretations have been placed by biographers upon these laconic lines of Lincoln. One of the most plausible is that of Jesse W. Weik, who said, "He believed there were other if not better ways of determining a man's fitness for a given task or position than the regulation test questions."*

LETTER TO SECRETARY OF WAR
EDWIN M. STANTON

Executive Mansion, November 11, 1863

DEAR SIR:

I personally wish Jacob Freese, of New Jersey, to be appointed colonel for a colored regiment, and this regardless of whether he can tell the exact shade of Julius Caesar's hair.

Yours, etc.,

A. LINCOLN

The Gettysburg Address

THE Gettysburg Address, which gained immortality for its author, and ranks as one of the greatest speeches in the English language, consists of only 10 sentences and 266 words, of which 193 are one-syllable words; and took but two short minutes to deliver.

ADDRESS AT THE GETTYSBURG NATIONAL CEMETERY

November 19, 1863

FOURSCORE and seven years ago our fathers brought forth on this continent a new nation, conceived in liberty, and dedicated to the proposition that all men are created equal.

Now we are engaged in a great civil war, testing whether that nation, or any nation so conceived and so dedicated, can long endure. We are met on a great battle-field of that war. We have come to dedicate a portion of that field as a final resting-place for those who here gave their lives that that nation might live. It is altogether fitting and proper that we should do this.

But, in a larger sense, we cannot dedicate—we cannot consecrate—we cannot hallow—this ground. The brave men, living and dead, who struggled here, have consecrated it far above our poor power to add or detract. The world will little note nor long remember what we say here, but it can never forget what they did here. It is for us, the living, rather, to be dedicated here to the unfinished work which they who fought here have thus far so nobly advanced. It is rather for us to be here dedicated to the great task remaining before us—that from these honored dead we take increased devotion to that cause for which they gave the last full measure of devotion; that we here highly resolve that these dead shall not have died in vain; that this nation, under God, shall have a new birth of freedom; and that government of the people, by the people, for the people, shall not perish from the earth.

". . . you could not have been excused to make
a short address, nor I a long one."

$\mathbb{F}$OLLOWING *the ceremonies at Gettysburg, Edward Everett, who was the principal speaker of the day, wrote to
Lincoln, "I should be glad if I could flatter myself that I came
as near the central idea of the occasion in two hours as you
did in two minutes."*

LETTER TO EDWARD EVERETT

Executive Mansion
Washington, D. C., November 20, 1863

$\mathbb{M}$Y DEAR SIR:
Your kind note of to-day is received.
In our respective parts yesterday, you could not
have been excused to make a short address, nor I a
long one. I am pleased to know that, in your judgment, the little I did say was not entirely a failure.
Of course I knew Mr. Everett would not fail,

and yet, while the whole discourse was eminently satisfactory, and will be of great value, there were passages in it which transcended my expectations.

The point made against the theory of the General Government being only an agency whose principals are the States, was new to me, and, as I think, is one of the best arguments for the national supremacy. The tribute to our noble women for their angel ministering to the suffering soldiers surpasses in its way, as do the subjects of it, whatever has gone before.

Our sick boy, for whom you kindly inquire, we hope is past the worst.

Your obedient servant,

A. LINCOLN

"An intelligent woman in deep distress. . . ."

O*N November 20, 1863 Lincoln wired Meade, "If there is a man by the name of King under sentence to be shot, please suspend execution till further order and send record." This explanatory letter followed.*

LETTER TO GENERAL GEORGE G. MEADE

Executive Mansion, November 20, 1863

M AJOR-GENERAL MEADE, ARMY OF POTOMAC:

An intelligent woman in deep distress, called this morning, saying her husband, a lieutenant in the Army of Potomac, was to be shot next Monday for desertion, and putting a letter in my hand, upon which I relied for particulars, she left without mentioning a name or other particular by which to identify the case. On opening the letter I found it equally vague, having nothing to identify by, except her own signature, which seems to be "Mrs. Anna S. King." I could not again find her. If you have a case which you shall think is probably the one intended, please apply my despatch of this morning to it.

A. Lincoln

". . . if the man does no wrong hereafter."

THE *principle expressed in this brief endorsement on a document submitted to the Secretary of War, premised Lincoln's whole theory of Reconstruction.*

INDORSEMENT ON DOCUMENT TO EDWIN M. STANTON

February 5, 1864

SUBMITTED TO THE SECRETARY OF WAR.
On principle I dislike an oath which requires a man to swear he has not done wrong. It rejects the Christian principle of forgiveness on terms of repentance. I think it is enough if the man does no wrong hereafter.

A. LINCOLN

"...I do not perceive occasion for a change."

IN *early 1864 a committee, headed by Senator Pomeroy of Kansas, created considerable clamor by publishing a letter vigorously attacking Lincoln and advocating Secretary of the Treasury Salmon P. Chase for the presidency. Somewhat taken aback, Chase wrote to Lincoln disclaiming any knowledge of the letter and saying, "If there is any thing in my action or position, which in your judgment will prejudice the public interest under my charge, I beg you to say so. I do not wish to administer the Treasury Department one day without your entire confidence." Lincoln deferred answering for a few days and then replied with his customary greatness of spirit.*

LETTER TO SALMON P. CHASE

Executive Mansion, February 29, 1864

MY DEAR SIR:
I would have taken time to answer yours of the 22d sooner, only that I did not sup-

pose any evil could result from the delay, especially as, by a note, I promptly acknowledged the receipt of yours, and promised a fuller answer. Now, on consideration, I find there is really very little to say. My knowledge of Mr. Pomeroy's letter having been made public came to me only the day you wrote but I had, in spite of myself, known of its existence several days before. I have not yet read it, and I think I shall not. I was not shocked or surprised by the appearance of the letter, because I had had knowledge of Mr. Pomeroy's committee, and of secret issues which I supposed came from it, and of secret agents who I supposed were sent out by it, for several weeks. I have known just as little of these things as my friends have allowed me to know. They bring the documents to me, but I do not read them; they tell me what they think fit to tell me, but I do not inquire for more. I fully concur with you that neither of us can be justly held responsible for what our respective friends may do without our instigation or countenance; and I assure you, as you have assured me, that no assault has been made upon you by my investigation or with my countenance. Whether you shall remain at the head of the Treasury Department is a question which I will not allow myself to con-

sider from any standpoint other than my judgment of the public service, and, in that view, I do
not perceive occasion for a change.

Yours truly,

A. LINCOLN

~~~~~~

"God *alone can claim it*."

~~~~~~

T̲WO *of Lincoln's best letters on slavery were written to Kentuckians—the first to Joshua Speed in 1855 and this one to A. G. Hodges nine years later.*

LETTER TO A. G. HODGES

Executive Mansion, April 4, 1864

M̲Y DEAR SIR:
You ask me to put in writing the substance of what I verbally said the other day in your presence, to Governor Bramlette and Senator Dixon. It was about as follows:

"I am naturally antislavery. If slavery is not wrong, nothing is wrong. I cannot remember when I did not so think and feel, and yet I have never understood that the presidency conferred upon me an unrestricted right to act officially upon this judgment and feeling. It was in the oath I took that I would, to the best of my ability, preserve, protect, and defend the Constitution of the United States. I could not take the office without taking the oath. Nor was it my view that I might take an oath to get power, and break the oath in using the power. I understood, too, that in ordinary civil administration this oath even forbade me to practically indulge my primary abstract judgment on the moral question of slavery. I had publicly declared this many times, and in many ways. And I aver that, to this day, I have done no official act in mere deference to my abstract judgment and feeling on slavery. I did understand, however, that my oath to preserve the Constitution to the best of my ability imposed upon me the duty of preserving, by every indispensable means, that government—that nation, of which that Constitution was the organic law. Was it possible to lose the nation and yet preserve the Constitution? By general law, life and limb must be protected, yet often a limb must be amputated to save a life; but a life is never wisely given to save a limb. I felt that measures otherwise unconstitutional might become lawful by becoming indispensable to the preservation of the Constitution through the preservation of the nation. Right or wrong, I assume this ground, and now avow it. I could not feel that, to the best of my ability, I had even tried to preserve the Constitution, if, to save slavery or any minor matter, I should permit the wreck of government, country, and Constitution all together. When, early in the war, General Fremont attempted military emancipation, I forbade it, because I did not then think it an indispensable necessity. When, a little later, General Cameron, then Secretary of War, suggested the arming of the blacks, I objected because I did not yet think it an indispensable necessity. When, still later, General Hunter attempted military emancipation, I again forbade it, because I did not yet think the indispensable necessity had come. When in March and May and July, 1862, I made earnest and successive appeals to the border States to favor compensated emancipation, I believed the indispensable necessity for military emancipation and arming the blacks would come unless averted by that measure. They declined the proposition, and I was, in my best judgment, driven to the alternative of either surrendering the Union, and with it the Constitution, or of laying strong hand upon the colored element. I chose the latter. In choosing it, I hoped for greater gain than loss; but of this, I was not entirely confident. More than a year of trial now shows no loss by it in our foreign relations, none in our home popular sentiment, none in our white military force—no loss by it anyhow or anywhere. On the contrary it shows a gain of quite a hundred and thirty thousand soldiers, seamen, and laborers. These are palpable facts, about which, as facts, there can be no caviling. We have the men; and we could not have had them without the measure.

"And now let any Union man who complains of the measure test himself by writing down in one line that he is for subduing the rebellion by force of arms; and in the next, that he is for taking these hundred and thirty thousand men from the Union side, and placing them where they would be but for the measure he condemns. If he cannot face his case so stated, it is only because he cannot face the truth."

I add a word which was not in the verbal conversation. In telling this tale I attempt no compliment to my own sagacity. I claim not to have controlled events, but confess plainly that events have controlled me. Now, at the end of three years' struggle, the nation's condition is not what either party, or any man, devised or expected. God alone can claim it. Whither it is tending seems plain. If God now wills the removal of a great wrong, and wills also that we of the North, as well as you of the South, shall pay fairly for our complicity in that wrong, impartial history will find therein new cause to attest and revere the justice and goodness of God.

Yours truly,

A. LINCOLN

Executive Mansion.

Washington, Jan, 5 ., 1865.

Hon. Sec. of War
  Dear Sir.

   Since parting with
you, it has occurred to me to
say that while Gen. Sher-
man's "get a good ready" is
appreciation, and is not to be
overlooked, time, now that
the enemy is wavering, is more
important than ever before.
Being on the down-hill,
somewhat confuse keep-
ing him going. Please say
so much to Genl. S.

      Yours truly, ——

      A. Lincoln

A newly discovered letter, not included in any of
the standard collections, in which Lincoln urges
that Sherman keep the enemy "going," while he is
on the "down-hill."

~~~~~~

". . . the wolf's dictionary has been repudiated."

~~~~~~

LINCOLN *frequently was entreated to speak at Sanitary Fairs, which resembled modern Red Cross Benefits. The speech he delivered at Baltimore was not, when considered as a whole, one of his best, but reflects in many passages the flash of his genius.*

ADDRESS AT BALTIMORE
APRIL 18, 1864

LADIES AND GENTLEMEN:
Calling to mind that we are in Baltimore, we cannot fail to note that the world moves. Looking upon these many people assembled here to serve, as they best may, the soldiers of the Union, it occurs at once that three years ago the same soldiers could not so much as pass through Baltimore. The change from then till now is both great and gratifying. Blessings on the brave men who have wrought the change, and the fair women who strive to reward them for it!

But Baltimore suggests more than could happen within Baltimore. The change within Baltimore is part only of a far wider change. When the war began, three years ago, neither party, nor any man, expected it would last till now. Each looked for the end, in some way, long ere to-day. Neither did any anticipate that domestic slavery would be much affected by the war. But here we are; the war has not ended, and slavery has been much affected—how much needs not now to be recounted. So true is it that man proposes and God disposes.

But we can see the past, though we may not claim to have directed it; and seeing it, in this case, we feel more hopeful and confident for the future.

The world has never had a good definition of the word liberty, and the American people, just now, are much in want of one. We all declare for liberty; but in using the same word we do not all mean the same thing. With some the word liberty may mean for each man to do as he pleases with himself, and the product of his labor; while with others the same word may mean for some men to do as they please with other men, and the product of other men's labor. Here are two, not only different, but incompatible things, called by the same name, liberty. And it follows that each of the things is, by the respective parties, called by two different and incompatible names—liberty and tyranny.

The shepherd drives the wolf from the sheep's throat, for which the sheep thanks the shepherd as his liberator, while the wolf denounces him for the same act, as the destroyer of liberty, especially as the sheep was a black one. Plainly, the sheep and the wolf are not agreed upon a definition of the word liberty; and precisely the same difference prevails to-day among us human creatures, even in the North, and all professing to love liberty. Hence we behold the process by which thousands are daily passing from under the yoke of bondage hailed by some as the advance of liberty, and be-wailed by others as the destruction of all liberty. Recently, as it seems, the people of Maryland have been doing something to define liberty, and thanks to them that, in what they have done, the wolf's dictionary has been repudiated.

It is not very becoming for one in my position to make speeches at great length; but there is an-other subject upon which I feel that I ought to say a word.

A painful rumor—true, I fear—has reached us of the massacre by the rebel forces at Fort Pillow, in the west end of Tennessee, on the Mississippi River, of some three hundred colored soldiers and white officers, who had just been overpowered by their assailants. There seems to be some anxiety in the public mind whether the government is doing its duty to the colored soldier, and to the service, at this point. At the beginning of the war, and for some time, the use of colored troops was not contemplated; and how the change of purpose was wrought I will not now take time to explain. Upon a clear conviction of duty I resolved to turn that element of strength to account; and I am responsible for it to the American people, to the Christian world, to history, and in my final account to God. Having determined to use the negro as a soldier, there is no way but to give him all the protection given to any other soldier. The difficulty is not in stating the principle, but in practically applying it. It is a mistake to suppose the government is indifferent to this matter, or is not doing the best it can in regard to it. We do not to-day know that a colored soldier, or white officer commanding colored soldiers, has been massacred by the rebels when made a prisoner. We fear it,—believe it, I may say,—but we do not know it. To take the life of one of their prisoners on the assumption that they murder ours, when it is short of certainty that they do murder ours, might be too serious, too cruel, a mistake. We are having the Fort Pillow affair thoroughly investigated; and such investigation will probably show conclusively how the truth is. If after all that has been said it shall turn out that there has been no massacre at Fort Pillow, it will be almost safe to say there has been none, and will be none, elsewhere. If there has been the massacre of three hundred there, or even the tenth part of three hundred, it will be conclusively proved; and being so proved, the retribution shall as surely come. It will be matter of grave consideration in what exact course to apply the retribution; but in the supposed case it must come.

www

"*. . . with a brave army and a just cause. . . .*"

wwwwwwwwwwwwwwwwwwwwwwwwwwwwwwwwwwwwwwwwwwwwwww

L‌INCOLN, *keenly understanding the psychology of his generals, knew just when to maintain a close surveillance and when, as in this case of General Grant, to invest them with complete authority.*

LETTER TO ULYSSES S. GRANT

Executive Mansion
Washington, April 30, 1864

L‌IEUTENANT GENERAL GRANT:
Not expecting to see you again before the Spring campaign opens, I wish to express, in this way, my entire satisfaction with what you have done up to this time, so far as I understand it. The particulars of your plans I neither know, or seek to know. You are vigilant and self-reliant, and, pleased with this, I wish not to obtrude any constraints or restraints upon you. While I am very

anxious that any great disaster, or the capture of our men in great numbers, shall be avoided, I know these points are less likely to escape your attention than they would be mine— If there is anything wanting which is within my power to give, do not fail to let me know it.

And now with a brave army, and a just cause, may God sustain you.

Yours very truly,

A. LINCOLN

LITTLE *suspecting that his own signature might some day prove to be of greater value, Lincoln sends along a "John Quincy Adams" autograph to the Secretary of War.*

LETTER TO EDWIN M. STANTON

June 14, 1864

MY DEAR STANTON:
Finding the above signature of Adams in an obscure place in the Mansion this morning and knowing of your weakness for oddities, I am sending it to you, hold on to it.—

It will no doubt be much more valuable some day.

Yours,

A. LINCOLN

~~~~~~

". . . notwithstanding any newspaper assaults."

~~~~~~

I*N the matter of granting pardons Lincoln was lenient to a degree that, it was feared, would affect the discipline of the army; but his firmness could not be shaken in cases where he felt no mercy was due.*

LETTER TO WILLIAM CULLEN BRYANT

Executive Mansion, June 27, 1864

M*Y DEAR SIR:*
        Yours of the twenty-fifth has just been handed me by the Secretary of the Navy. The tone of the letter, rather than any direct statement in it, impresses me as a complaint that Mr. Henderson should have been removed from office, and arrested; coupled with the single suggestion that he be restored if he shall establish his innocence.

I know absolutely nothing of the case except as follows: Monday last, Mr. Welles came to me with the letter of dismissal already written, saying he thought proper to show it to me before sending it. I asked him the charges, which he stated in a general way. With as much emphasis as I could, I said: "Are you entirely certain of his guilt?" He answered that he was, to which I replied: "Then send the letter."

Whether Mr. Henderson was a supporter of my second nomination, I neither knew nor inquired, nor even thought of. I shall be very glad indeed if he shall, as you anticipate, establish his innocence; or, to state it more strongly and properly, "if the government shall fail to establish his guilt." I believe, however, the man who made the affidavit was of as spotless reputation as Mr. Henderson, until he was arrested on what his friends insist was outrageously insufficient evidence. I know the entire city government of Washington, with many other respectable citizens, appealed to me in his behalf as a greatly injured gentleman.

While the subject is up, may I ask whether the "Evening Post" has not assailed me for supposed too lenient dealing with persons charged with fraud and crime? And that in cases of which the "Post" could know but little of the facts? I shall certainly deal as leniently with Mr. Henderson as

I have felt it my duty to deal with others, notwithstanding any newspaper assaults.

Your obedient servant,

A. LINCOLN

"... a point of mutual embarrassment. ..."

THREE *times Salmon P. Chase had resigned as Secretary of the Treasury; three times a patient Lincoln had persuaded him to reconsider; but when Chase handed in his resignation for the fourth time, Lincoln decided it was time to "call quits."*

LETTER TO SALMON P. CHASE

Executive Mansion, June 30, 1864

MY DEAR SIR:

Your resignation of the office of Secretary of the Treasury sent me yesterday is accepted. Of all I have said in commendation of your ability and fidelity I have nothing to unsay; and yet you and I have reached a point of mutual embarrassment in our official relations which it seems cannot be overcome or longer sustained consistently with the public service.

Your obedient servant,

A. LINCOLN

"I propose continuing myself to be the judge. . . ."

WHEN *General Halleck, Chief of Staff, virtually demanded the dismissal of Postmaster-General Blair, Lincoln
refused, saying, "I propose continuing myself to be the judge
as to when a member of the Cabinet shall be dismissed." Two
months later, seeing that the breach between his Cabinet members could never be healed, Lincoln asked for Blair's resignation.*

LETTER TO EDWIN M. STANTON

Executive Mansion, July 14, 1864

SIR:
Your note of to-day inclosing General
Halleck's letter of yesterday relative to offensive
remarks supposed to have been made by the Postmaster-General concerning the military officers on
duty about Washington is received. The general's
letter in substance demands of me that if I approve

the remarks I shall strike the names of those officers from the rolls; and that if I do not approve
them the Postmaster-General shall be dismissed
from the Cabinet.

Whether the remarks were really made I do not
know, nor do I suppose such knowledge is necessary to a correct response. If they were made, I do
not approve them; and yet, under the circumstances, I would not dismiss a member of the Cabinet therefor. I do not consider what may have been
hastily said in a moment of vexation at so severe
a loss is sufficient ground for so grave a step. Be-
sides this, truth is generally the best vindication
against slander. I propose continuing to be myself
the judge as to when a member of the Cabinet
shall be dismissed.

Yours truly,

A. LINCOLN

~~~~~~

"Hold on with a bull-dog grip. . . ."

~~~~~~

W̲HEN *a number of State Governors had appealed to General Grant to release troops to suppress draft uprisings, Grant flatly refused to weaken his lines and was strongly backed in his decision by the Commander-in-Chief.*

TELEGRAM TO ULYSSES S. GRANT

Executive Mansion, Washington, D. C.
August 17, 1864, 10:30 A.M.

L̲IEUTENANT-GENERAL GRANT, City
Point, Va.:

I have seen your despatch expressing your unwillingness to break your hold where you are. Neither am I willing. Hold on with a bull-dog grip, and chew and choke as much as possible.

A. LINCOLN

Secret Pledge

AFTER *his reëlection Lincoln drew from his desk drawer this sealed memorandum, which he had asked his Cabinet members to sign, unseen, several months before.*

SECRET MEMORANDUM
SIGNED BY CABINET MEMBERS

Executive Mansion
Washington, August 23, 1864

THIS morning, as for some days past, it seems exceedingly probable that this administration will not be reëlected. Then it will be my duty to so cooperate with the President-elect as to save the Union between the election and the inauguration; as he will have secured his election on such ground that he cannot possibly save it afterward.

A. LINCOLN

". . . inflammatory appeals to your passions
and your prejudices."

L INCOLN *addresses a few words of caution to an Ohio regiment, returning home long after their original 3-months term of enlistment had expired.*

ADDRESS TO THE 148TH OHIO REGIMENT
AUGUST 31, 1864

S OLDIERS OF THE 148TH OHIO:

I am most happy to meet you on this occasion. I understand that it has been your honorable privilege to stand, for a brief period, in the defense of your country, and that now you are on your way to your homes. I congratulate you, and those who are waiting to bid you welcome home from the war; and permit me in the name of the people to thank you for the part you have taken in this struggle for the life of the nation. You are soldiers of the republic, everywhere honored and respected. Whenever I appear before a body of soldiers I feel tempted to talk to them of the nature of the struggle in which we are engaged. I look upon it as an attempt on the one hand to overwhelm and destroy the national existence, while on our part we are striving to maintain the government and institutions of our fathers, to enjoy them ourselves, and transmit them to our children and our children's children forever.

To do this the constitutional administration of our government must be sustained, and I beg of you not to allow your minds or your hearts to be diverted from the support of all necessary measures for that purpose, by any miserable picayune arguments addressed to your pockets, or inflammatory appeals made to your passions and your prejudices.

It is vain and foolish to arraign this man or that for the part he has taken or has not taken, and to hold the government responsible for his acts. In no administration can there be perfect equality of action and uniform satisfaction rendered by all.

But this government must be preserved in spite of the acts of any man or set of men. It is worthy of your every effort. Nowhere in the world is presented a government of so much liberty and equality. To the humblest and poorest amongst us are held out the highest privileges and positions. The present moment finds me at the White House, yet there is as good a chance for your children as there was for my father's.

Again I admonish you not to be turned from your stern purpose of defending our beloved country and its free institutions by any arguments urged by ambitious and designing men, but to stand fast for the Union and the old flag.

Soldiers, I bid you God-speed to your homes.

"... opposed to both war and oppression. ..."

Recognizing *the "hard dilemma" which confronts the Quakers by reason of their faith, Lincoln points out that "they can only practically oppose oppression by war."*

LETTER TO ELIZA P. GURNEY

Executive Mansion, September 4, 1864

MY ESTEEMED FRIEND:

I have not forgotten—probably never shall forget—the very impressive occasion when yourself and friends visited me on a Sabbath forenoon two years ago. Nor has your kind letter, written nearly a year later, ever been forgotten. In all it has been your purpose to strengthen my reliance on God. I am much indebted to the good Christian people of the country for their constant prayers and consolations; and to no one of them more than to yourself. The purposes of the Almighty are perfect, and must prevail, though we erring mortals may fail to accurately perceive them in advance. We hoped for a happy termination of this terrible war long before this; but God knows best, and has ruled otherwise. We shall yet acknowledge his wisdom, and our own error therein. Meanwhile we must work earnestly in the best lights he gives us, trusting that so working still conduces to the great ends he ordains. Surely he intends some great good to follow this mighty convulsion, which no mortal could make, and no mortal could stay. Your people, the Friends, have had, and are having, a very great trial. On principle and faith opposed to both war and oppression, they can only practically oppose oppression by war. In this hard dilemma some have chosen one horn, and some the other. For those appealing to me on conscientious grounds, I have done, and shall do, the best I could and can, in my own conscience, under my oath to the law. That you believe this I doubt not; and, believing it, I shall still receive for our country and myself your earnest prayers to our Father in heaven.

Your sincere friend,

A. Lincoln

"The time has come."

Having *decided that a Cabinet-split can be avoided in no other way, Lincoln assumes the unpleasant task of asking for the resignation of his friend Montgomery Blair.*

LETTER TO POSTMASTER-GENERAL MONTGOMERY BLAIR

Executive Mansion, September 23, 1864

My dear sir:

You have generously said to me more than once that whenever your resignation could be a relief to me it was at my disposal. The time has come. You very well know that this proceeds from no dissatisfaction of mine with you personally or officially. Your uniform kindness has been unsurpassed by that of any friend; and while it is true that the war does not so greatly add to the difficulties of your department as to those of some others, it is yet much to say, as I most truly can, that in the three years and a half during which you have administered the general post-office, I remember no single complaint against you in connection therewith.

Yours,

A. LINCOLN

*". . . whether any government not too strong
for the liberties of its people. . . ."*

Sᴘᴇᴀᴋɪɴɢ *to a cheering crowd after his victorious reëlection,
Lincoln put his finger on a principle which is both the strength
and weakness of a Democracy.*

RESPONSE TO SERENADE
NOVEMBER 10, 1864

IT has long been a grave question whether any
government, not too strong for the liberties
of its people, can be strong enough to maintain its
existence in great emergencies. On this point the
present rebellion brought our republic to a severe
test, and a presidential election occurring in regular course during the rebellion, added not a little
to the strain.

If the loyal people united were put to the utmost of their strength by the rebellion, must they
not fail when divided and partially paralyzed by a

political war among themselves? But the election was a necessity. We cannot have free government without elections; and if the rebellion could force us to forego or postpone a national election, it might fairly claim to have already conquered and ruined us. The strife of the election is but human nature practically applied to the facts of the case. What has occurred in this case must ever recur in similar cases. Human nature will not change. In any future great national trial, compared with the men of this, we shall have as weak and as strong, as silly and as wise, as bad and as good. Let us, therefore, study the incidents of this as philosophy to learn wisdom from, and none of them as wrongs to be revenged. But the election, along with its incidental and undesirable strife, has done good too. It has demonstrated that a people's government can sustain a national election in the midst of a great civil war. Until now, it has not been known to the world that this was a possibility. It shows, also, how sound and how strong we still are. It shows that, even among candidates of the same party, he who is most devoted to the Union and most opposed to treason can receive most of the people's votes. It shows, also, to the extent yet known, that we have more men now than we had when the war began. Gold is good in its place, but living, brave, patriotic men are better than gold.

But the rebellion continues, and now that the election is over, may not all having a common interest reunite in a common effort to save our common country? For my own part, I have striven and shall strive to avoid placing any obstacle in the way. So long as I have been here I have not willingly planted a thorn in any man's bosom. While I am deeply sensible to the high compliment of a reëlection, and duly grateful, as I trust, to Almighty God for having directed my countrymen to a right conclusion, as I think, for their own good, it adds nothing to my satisfaction that any other man may be disappointed or pained by the result.

May I ask those who have not differed from me to join with me in this same spirit toward those who have? And now let me close by asking three hearty cheers for our brave soldiers and seamen and their gallant and skilful commanders.

Lincoln's Letter to Mrs. Bixby

FEW *will disagree with George S. Boutwell, delegate to the Convention that nominated Lincoln, and Congressman in the most critical years of the war, who said, "All history and all literature may be searched and in vain, for a funeral tribute so touching, so comprehensive, so fortunate in expression as this."*

LETTER TO MRS. BIXBY

Executive Mansion
November 21, 1864

DEAR MADAM:

I have been shown in the files of the War Department a statement of the Adjutant-General of Massachusetts that you are the mother of five sons who have died gloriously on the field of battle. I feel how weak and fruitless must be any word of mine which should attempt to beguile you from the grief of a loss so overwhelming. But I cannot refrain from tendering you the consolation that may be found in the thanks of the Republic they died to save. I pray that our heavenly Father may assuage the anguish of your bereavement, and leave you only the cherished memory of the loved and lost, and the solemn pride that must be yours to have laid so costly a sacrifice upon the altar of freedom.

Yours very sincerely and respectfully,

ABRAHAM LINCOLN

~~~~~~

". . . the incident at the polls. . . ."

~~~~~~

THE *President thanks Deacon Phillips of Sturbridge, Massachusetts, not only for casting his vote for him, but for having exercised his right of suffrage at every Presidential election since the country was founded.*

LETTER TO JOHN PHILLIPS

Executive Mansion, November 21, 1864

MY DEAR SIR:

I have heard of the incident at the polls in your town, in which you acted so honorable a part, and I take the liberty of writing to you to express my personal gratitude for the compliment paid me by the suffrage of a citizen so venerable.

The example of such devotion to civic duties in one whose days have already been extended an average lifetime beyond the Psalmist's limit, cannot but be valuable and fruitful. It is not for myself only, but for the country which you have in your sphere served so long and so well, that I thank you.

Your friend and servant,

ABRAHAM LINCOLN

". . . when I have nothing to talk about."

LINCOLN *adheres to his lifelong principle of wasting neither his own words nor his listeners' time.*

RESPONSE TO SERENADE
DECEMBER 6, 1864

FRIENDS AND FELLOW-CITIZENS:
I believe I shall never be old enough to speak without embarrassment when I have nothing to talk about. I have no good news to tell you, and yet I have no bad news to tell. We have talked of elections until there is nothing more to say about them. The most interesting news we now have is from Sherman. We all know where he went in, but I can't tell where he will come out. I will now close by proposing three cheers for General Sherman and his army.

~~~~~~

"... thanks for your Christmas gift. ..."

~~~~~~

LINCOLN *thanks General Sherman for his Christmas gift —the capture of Savannah—making sure to reserve none of the credit for himself.*

LETTER TO WILLIAM TECUMSEH SHERMAN

Executive Mansion, December 26, 1864

MY DEAR GENERAL SHERMAN:
Many, many thanks for your Christmas gift, the capture of Savannah.

When you were about leaving Atlanta for the Atlantic coast, I was anxious, if not fearful; but feeling that you were the better judge, and remembering that "nothing risked, nothing gained," I did not interfere. Now, the undertaking being a success, the honor is all yours; for I believe none of us went further than to acquiesce.

And taking the work of General Thomas into

the count, as it should be taken, it is indeed a great success. Not only does it afford the obvious and immediate military advantages; but in showing to the world that your army could be divided, putting the stronger part to an important new service, and yet leaving enough to vanquish the old opposing force of the whole,—Hood's army,— it brings those who sat in darkness to see a great light. But what next?

I suppose it will be safe if I leave General Grant and yourself to decide.

Please make my grateful acknowledgments to your whole army—officers and men.

Yours very truly,

A. LINCOLN

~~~~~~

"... get a good ready. ..."

~~~~~~

SEEING *the end drawing near, Lincoln hopes that General Sherman will keep the enemy "going."*

LETTER TO EDWIN M. STANTON

Executive Mansion
Washington, Jan. 5, 1865

HON. SEC. OF WAR

DEAR SIR:
    Since parting with you, it has occurred to me to say that while Gen. Sherman's *"get a good ready"* is appreciated, and is not to be overlooked, *time,* now that the enemy is wavering, is more important than ever before. Being on the down-hill, somewhat confirms keeping him going. Please say so much to Gen. S.

Yours truly,

A. LINCOLN

~~~~~~

"... as though I was not President...."

~~~~~~

THIS *letter to General Grant was written upon one of the extremely rare occasions when Lincoln sought a personal favor for himself. As was the case with so many of Lincoln's writings, it was flawless in sentiment, if not in syntax.*

LETTER TO ULYSSES S. GRANT

Executive Mansion, January 19, 1865

LIEUTENANT-GENERAL GRANT:

Please read and answer this letter as though I was not President, but only a friend. My son, now in his twenty-second year, having graduated at Harvard, wishes to see something of the war before it ends. I do not wish to put him in the ranks, nor yet to give him a commission, to which those who have already served long are better entitled and better qualified to hold. Could he, without embarrassment to you or detriment to the service, go into your military family with some nominal rank, I, and not the public, furnishing his necessary means? If no, say so without the least hesitation, because I am as anxious and as deeply interested that you shall not be encumbered as you can be yourself.

Yours truly,

A. LINCOLN

~~~~~~

"... with a distrust of my own ability. ..."

~~~~~~

LINCOLN *responds, with his usual diffidence, to the Committee informing him of the result of the Electoral count.*

REPLY TO CONGRESSIONAL COMMITTEE
FEBRUARY 9, 1865*

WITH deep gratitude to my countrymen for this mark of their confidence; with a distrust of my own ability to perform the duty required under the most favorable circumstances, and now rendered doubly difficult by existing national perils; yet with a firm reliance on the strength of our free government, and the eventual loyalty of the people to the just principles, upon which it is founded, and above all with an unshaken faith in the Supreme Ruler of nations, I accept this trust. Be pleased to signify this to the respective Houses of Congress.

* *Although the letter bears this date in many standard collections, Paul M. Angle has uncovered evidence which incontrovertibly establishes the date as February 26, 1861—at the time of Lincoln's first election.*

ww

"With malice toward none. . . ."

wwwwwwwwwwwwwwwwwwwwwwwwwwwwwwwwwwwwwwwwwwwwwwwwwwww

LORD CURZON, *Chancellor of the University of Oxford, named as the "three supreme masterpieces of English Eloquence" the Toast of William Pitt after the Victory of Trafalgar, Lincoln's Gettysburg Speech, and Lincoln's Second Inaugural Address. Dr. Louis A. Warren interestingly observes that "One-third of the entire address, or to be exact, 267 of the 702 words were direct quotations from the Bible and words of application made to them."*

SECOND INAUGURAL ADDRESS
MARCH 4, 1865

FELLOW-COUNTRYMEN:

At this second appearing to take the oath of the presidential office, there is less occasion for an extended address than there was at the first. Then a statement, somewhat in detail, of a course to be pursued, seemed fitting and proper. Now, at the expiration of four years, during which public declarations have been constantly called forth on every point and phase of the great contest which still absorbs the attention and engrosses the energies of the nation, little that is new could be presented. The progress of our arms, upon which all else chiefly depends, is as well known to the public as to myself; and it is, I trust, reasonably satisfactory and encouraging to all. With high hope for the future, no prediction in regard to it is ventured.

On the occasion corresponding to this four years ago, all thoughts were anxiously directed to an impending civil war. All dreaded it—all sought to avert it. While the inaugural address was being delivered from this place, devoted altogether to saving the Union without war, insurgent agents were in the city seeking to destroy it without war —seeking to dissolve the Union, and divide effects, by negotiation. Both parties deprecated war; but one of them would make war rather than let the nation survive; and the other would accept war rather than let it perish. And the war came.

One-eighth of the whole population were colored slaves, not distributed generally over the Union, but localized in the Southern part of it. These slaves constituted a peculiar and powerful interest. All knew that this interest was, somehow, the cause of the war. To strengthen, perpetuate, and extend this interest was the object for which the insurgents would rend the Union, even by war; while the government claimed no right to do more than to restrict the territorial enlargement of it.

Neither party expected for the war the magnitude or the duration which it has already attained. Neither anticipated that the cause of the conflict might cease with, or even before, the conflict itself should cease. Each looked for an easier triumph, and a result less fundamental and astounding. Both read the same Bible, and pray to the same God; and each invokes his aid against the other. It may seem strange that any men should dare to ask a just God's assistance in wringing their bread from the sweat of other men's faces; but let us judge not, that we be not judged. The prayers of both could not be answered—that of neither has been answered fully.

The Almighty has his own purposes. "Woe unto the world because of offenses! for it must needs be that offenses come; but woe to that man by whom the offense cometh." If we shall suppose that American slavery is one of those offenses which, in the providence of God, must needs come, but which, having continued through his appointed time, he now wills to remove, and that he gives to both North and South this terrible war, as the woe due to those by whom the offense came, shall we discern therein any departure from those divine attributes which the believers in a living God always ascribe to him? Fondly do we hope—fervently do we pray—that this mighty scourge of war may speedily pass away. Yet, if God wills that it continue until all the wealth piled by the bondman's two hundred and fifty years of unrequited toil shall be sunk, and until every drop of blood drawn with the lash shall be paid by another drawn with the sword, as was said three thousand years ago, so still it must be said, "The judgments of the Lord are true and righteous altogether."

With malice toward none; with charity for all; with firmness in the right, as God gives us to see the right, let us strive on to finish the work we are in; to bind up the nation's wounds; to care for him who shall have borne the battle, and for his widow, and his orphan—to do all which may achieve and cherish a just and lasting peace among ourselves, and with all nations.

〜〜〜〜〜〜〜〜〜〜〜〜〜〜〜〜〜〜〜〜〜〜〜〜〜〜〜〜〜〜〜〜〜〜〜〜

"It is a truth which I thought needed to be told. . . ."

〜〜〜〜〜〜〜〜〜〜〜〜〜〜〜〜〜〜〜〜〜〜〜〜〜〜〜〜〜〜〜〜〜〜〜〜

F EW *letters give a better insight into the mind and soul of Lincoln than this short classic, written to Thurlow Weed, who had complimented the President upon his Second Inaugural Address.*

LETTER TO THURLOW WEED

Executive Mansion, March 15, 1865

D EAR MR. WEED:

Every one likes a compliment. Thank you for yours on my little notification speech and on the recent inaugural address. I expect the latter to wear as well as—perhaps better than—anything I have produced; but I believe it is not immediately popular. Men are not flattered by being shown that there has been a difference of purpose between the Almighty and them. To deny it, however, in this case, is to deny that there is a God governing the world. It is a truth which I thought needed to be told, and, as whatever of humiliation there is in it falls most directly on myself, I thought others might afford for me to tell it.

Truly yours,

A. LINCOLN

~~~~~~

"Let the thing be pressed."

~~~~~~

IN *a telegram that is almost epigrammatic, Lincoln urges General Grant to make "the final effort."*

TELEGRAM TO ULYSSES S. GRANT

Headquarters Armies of the U. S.,
City Point, April 7, 1865, 11 A.M.

LIEUTENANT-GENERAL GRANT:
Gen. Sheridan says "If the thing is pressed I think that Lee will surrender." Let the *thing* be pressed.

A. LINCOLN

"The President's last, shortest, and best speech."

ONE day in December of 1864 Lincoln handed a sheet of paper to newspaper correspondent Noah Brooks. On it was written the following message, with the heading heavily undescored.

The President's last, shortest, and best speech

ON Thursday of last week two ladies from Tennessee came before the President asking the release of their husbands held as prisoners of war at Johnson's Island— They were put off till Friday, when they came again; and were again put off to Saturday— At each of the interviews one of the ladies urged that her husband was a religious man— On Saturday the President ordered the release of the prisoners, and then said to this lady "You say your husband is a religious man; tell him when you meet him, that I say I am not much of a judge of religion, but that, in my opinion, the religion that sets men to rebel and fight against their government, because, as they think, that government does not sufficiently help *some* men to eat their bread in the sweat of *other* men's faces, is not the sort of religion upon which people can get to heaven!"

A. LINCOLN